[handwritten inscription: "To Lucy with thanks"]

Argyll Street

One man's journey from the pit to the front line

[handwritten signature]

JON MOORTHORPE

[handwritten: "9 February 2020"]

This is a historical novel based on the life of the author's Great
Uncle William Gregory. The main characters, events, locations, and
organizations are factual, whereas other characters and detailed
incidents are largely the product of the author's imagination.

ISBN: 978-1-6847-1089-8 (sc)
ISBN: 978-1-6847-1090-4 (hc)
ISBN: 978-1-6847-1091-1 (e)

Library of Congress Control Number: 2019914786

Lulu Publishing Services rev. date: 10/28/2019

In remembrance of the brave men of the 25th Battalion Nova Scotia Rifles (Cape Breton Highlanders) who served on the Western Front in World War One.

CONTENTS

Contents

ACKNOWLEDGEMENTS

A copy of this book is also held
by the British Library
Cover design by http://www.book-design.co.uk
Author website http://www.jonmoorthorpe.org
Photographic images by : Wigan Archives
Service, Library and Archives Canada

THIS BOOK RELIES on facts resulting from the many years of painstaking research carried out by my sister, Margaret. I also wish to show my appreciation to my partner Jean for her unfailing patience; Dorothy Makinson of Aspull for her advice on family history; Ken Lees for his vast knowledge of the Somme battlefields, including Lens and Hill 70; his wife Karen for her advice and hospitality during our 2016 visit; Lieutenant Colonel R. G. Gallant CD; John Clark, former RSM and now curator of the Regimental Museum; Sister Georgette Gregory CSJ; Dominique Groeseneken; Julie Forsyth for editing and formatting; Andrew Nowell of the *Wigan Post*; Alex Miller of the Wigan Archives Service; Garry D. Shutlack of the Nova Scotia Archives; Christine Hammacott at The Art of Communication; Alan Hyatt for his advice on WWI Royal Flying Corps airfields; Dan Jones for his design and formatting advice; Chris Forsey of Blackshire ASP; and members of Chindi, Worthy Words, and the Bognor Regis Writers Group; Canadian Roots UK; Queen Alexandra's Hospital Home for Veterans; Elly Donovan PR.

For their support during the edit and reviewing activities, I owe an equal debt of gratitude to Madeline Dent, Maurice and Sue Belgrave, Mike Fescina, Andy Burt, Mike Popham, Sid West, Fay Lewis, Jeremy Good, Philip and Amy Sykes, Richard and Sue Jeal, Peter and Sue Crane, Allyson Scanlon, and Lucy Peel. I hope that I may be forgiven by any I may have missed.

INTRODUCTION

THE RESEARCH FOR this book led to a better understanding of the hardships suffered by working-class families throughout the United Kingdom in the nineteenth and the first part of the twentieth centuries. This period in history, post-Industrial Revolution, saw a significant increase in the demand for skilled labour, raw materials, and manufactured goods—particularly for those used in the weapons supplied to armies fighting wars in all corners of Europe.

In the coal mining industry, it was common practice for very young boys and girls to be employed underground moving tubs of coal many hundreds of yards to the pit bottom where they were loaded onto a wooden platform then raised to the surface. The period covered in this book saw children, now from the age of ten, employed underground as either a *thrutcher*, who would push the filled coal tub from behind, or as a *drawer*, pulling the tub from the front while wearing a leather belt around the waist with a chain passing through the legs and attached to the underside of the tub.

The Mines Act of 1842 introduced provisions regarding the employment of children and women in coal mines and in particular that:

• No female was to be employed underground
• No boy under the age of ten was to work underground

However, these requirements imposed great financial hardship on families who had previously relied on the income from sending all their children to work at the pit. As a result, these new statutory rulings were frequently ignored when, for example, girls dressed in men's clothing or the larger boys lied about their age. It was, therefore, not surprising that the pit management invariably turned a blind eye to this practice when, in truth, they knew all the families in the village.

In Lancashire, the Gregory family lived in a two-bedroom terraced house in Stanley Road Aspull, a small village where employment mainly depended on coal mining at the Aspull Moor Number five pit, at Dicconson's Cotton Mill, or at the Albion Iron

Works. The majority of housing belonged to the pit owner, and the weekly rent was deducted from a worker's earnings.

In March 1879, Ellen Gregory gave birth to a baby boy, the fifth child in the family that would eventually number nine in total. As usual, Ellen's best friend, Bea Hardacre, helped with the birth. The new baby was named William.

From the time William started to walk, his elder brother Harry assumed charge of mentoring his younger sibling, teaching him all those things in life that seemed important to a boy of seven, including, for example, kicking a football, a skill that proved extremely challenging for a two-year-old. The two brothers soon became inseparable, and this close bond was to continue for the rest of their lives.

William left school on the Friday following his tenth birthday in March 1889, and the following Monday was to be his first shift at the pit working as Dad's thrutcher.

Queen Victoria died on 22 January 1901, having reigned for sixty-three years, at the time the longest-serving monarch in British history

On 25 July 1906 William, now a married man aged twenty-seven, emigrated to Canada and sailed from Liverpool, bound for Quebec on board the liner

SS *Empress of Ireland*, which had only been in service since January of that year.

For readers' information

In the early hours of 29 May 1914, the *Empress* was in a collision with the Norwegian ship SS *Storstad* on the St Lawrence River, and the *Empress* sank, with the loss of 1,012 lives. This incident represented the greatest number of deaths in any Canadian maritime accident in peacetime.

CHAPTER 1

First Shift

HARRY SHOOK WILLIAM'S shoulder for the second time. "Come on, William. Look sharpish. It's half past five and time to get up for work. If you don't get a move on, Dad will clip your ear for sure."

"But I'm so tired, our Harry. Just a little bit longer." William turned on his side.

Five minutes later, Dad called up the stairs. "For goodness' sake, wake up boy! Look lively now. This will not do." Dad was normally very quietly spoken, so the stern tone of his voice had an instant effect. William swung his legs out of bed in a second. "Our Harry's downstairs, already dressed and ready to go, so you've no time now for any breakfast. You'll have to take some bread to chew on the way up to the pit."

"I'm sorry, Dad. I'm coming down now."

"Then be sure you are. Lucky lad that you are,

with our Harry's long trousers he's outgrown, the cap Mam made, and the new clogs as well."

Downstairs on the kitchen table, there were four Tommy cans (see "Terminology"), which Mam had filled with bread and cheese last night. Three were for Dad, Harry, and William, and the fourth was for Mary when she went to work on the pit brow later. They each filled a water bottle from the outside tap. Dad finished his tea, opened the back door, and the two boys followed him out into Stanley Road.

It was cold and damp out with a few spots of rain to begin with. Then by the time they reached the bottom of the street, it had turned to a steady drizzle, and they were almost soaked through to the skin. They had been joined by others as they went along, and William was finding it hard going to keep up with them all.

Whilst he found it difficult to follow much of what the men talked about, he did find it funny that, as each new man stepped out of their front door, they all greeted each other with the same expression. "Damp out this morning, eh? Fine weather for ducks I'd say."

He soon learned that they said much the same most mornings. Then of course they would; this was typical Lancashire weather.

As they approached the pit gates, William could see a large crowd of men in the yard beyond. He had thought there would be others he would recognise from school who were also joining their first shift but didn't see anyone he knew.

Harry was walking alongside talking to Jimmy Simm. The two had been pals ever since their schooldays, and Jimmy had been Dad's thrutcher until last Saturday morning's shift. Today he was starting as a drawer for Mr Cooper, making way for William's first day at work.

Jimmy waved at Dad. "Mornin', Mr Gregory."

"Mornin', Jimmy. I only hope your timekeeping improves now you're with Mr Cooper. He's not going to be as easy as me to work for. You know you can't afford to get on the wrong side of either Eric Cooper or Mr Grimshaw; not a happy pair, those two."

William knew Mr Cooper, who lived further down Stanley Road but didn't know anyone called Grimshaw, so he tugged Harry's sleeve. "Who's this Mr Grimshaw, Harry?"

"The banksman." Harry pointed towards the head of the queue ahead.

"What's the banksman, Harry?"

"See the big man at the front with the brown overcoat and bowler hat?"

3

William nodded.

"Well, he's the one checking each man waiting to go down in the cage. He's responsible for everything and everyone going underground and everything coming back up, as well as directing the winding gear operator. During the day, his mate keeps the record of coal tubs up and down the shaft. In other words, the banksman is in charge of everything around here. He's the owner's main man, I'd say. Right, Jimmy?"

"Dead right, Harry. Now you make sure you never get the wrong side of him, William. Grim by name, grimmer by nature. So stay well clear's my advice."

"Thanks, Jimmy. I will."

They shuffled slowly towards the front of the queue until it was their turn next. Dad pushed William in front of him, at the same time showing the banksman his number tag. Mr Grimshaw was the biggest man William had ever seen. He ran his finger down the list attached to his board. "Now. Who do we have here then? Another young Gregory I take it?"

"It is," Dad replied. "William's his name."

Mr Grimshaw rummaged through his coat pocket and handed a new identity tag to William. "There you are, young man—number 2365. Remember that and guard it as though your very life depended on it. It may well do one of these days. Through you go now. And stay close to your dad."

William held onto the sleeve of Dad's jacket as they squeezed tightly onto the wooden platform. Waiting for the cage to start its descent, no one spoke for a couple of minutes. Then the quiet was interrupted by a loud voice. "My God. Was that you, Shelley? The bloody place stinks enough without your farts adding to it."

"You know me, Ted," Shelley replied. "Silent but deadly."

So, this was the kind of thing the men talked about. William put his hand over his mouth to stifle a giggle. It sounded so funny. Harry grinned and nodded at Dad, who had turned his back, ignoring the banter causing such childish humour.

"I don't know what you find so funny boy. You wouldn't think so if you were standing where I am."

William assumed it must be Ted speaking, whoever Ted was.

Then the cage started to move. William could still see Mr Grimshaw, who was waving to someone high above their heads, and then suddenly they were in total darkness. The creaking, groaning, and strange scraping kinds of sounds were quite frightening, and

William wondered whether it had ever fallen to the bottom. It obviously didn't worry any of the others, as this was all part of the daily routine for them. The movement of the cage was gradually slowing as it got nearer to the bottom. Then with a loud thud, they had obviously arrived. Someone lifted the outer crossbar, and then everyone was pushing and shoving to get off. Some went to the left and some to the right. Harry put his hand on William's shoulder, guiding him to the right after Dad. He waved back at Jimmy, "See ya later, Jimmy. Good luck."

The tunnel was mostly in darkness, other than the occasional oil lamp or candlelight, and William stumbled two or three times as the roadway was pretty rough and slippery underfoot. Every time he fell, Harry grabbed his jacket and hauled him back onto his feet, while Dad called out, "Hurry along, you two. Wasted time is costing me money!"

It was only about a hundred yards from the bottom that they eventually stopped at the entrance to a tunnel about six feet wide and six high on the left. Harry took two candles from his pocket, lit them, and placed them on a ledge next to the tools. Dad took a pick and a shovel and disappeared through the hole in the face, no more than four feet high.

After a short while, he called out, "Coal!" and

started to shovel lumps of coal back from the face. After about fifteen minutes, their first tub was full, and William was pushing his first full load, with Harry pulling from the front.

By the end of the shift, Harry and William had filled and moved four tubs back to the bottom and on to the cage. Dad was pleased with the first day's work, "Well done, boys. Five or six a day by the end of the week then, Harry?"

"Yes, Dad. We'll be improving each day as the week goes on. To say it's his first shift, our William did very well."

Dad put his arm around William's shoulder. "Not bad at all for your first shift, son. You'll soon get used to it. On the way home, I think we'll have a quick pint at the Ivy. Our Harry can go in with me now he's sixteen, but you must have a lemonade and sit outside. We won't be long."

The quick one turned out to be two. And by the time they left the Ivy an hour later, they found William curled up on the bench outside, fast asleep.

Ellen and John Gregory in Aspull, 1900

Bad Man / Best Man

Bea Hardacre had been Ellen Gregory's best friend ever since they were at school together. And although they weren't related, as so often was the case, the children knew their mother's closest friend as Aunty. Bea had four children under the age of ten.

It was now nearly two years since Bea's husband, Edwin had died in a gas explosion at the pit. For the first twelve months or so after, she'd rarely left the house other than to go up Stanley Road to visit Ellen. However, for the past six months, she had enjoyed visiting her sister in Blackburn at least once a month. When she did so, she'd ask either Maggie or Mary to babysit until five o'clock, which was the children's' normal bedtime. Then, as he was doing now, William would often take over listening out for them until she returned home on the last bus, generally about ten o'clock.

"Have they been good for you, William?"

"Good as gold, Aunty Bea. Maggie waited until they were fast asleep, and not a sound from them since."

"Well, you'd best be on your way home, William. Your mam will be wondering where you've got to. Thanks again for looking after the little ones for me. I wouldn't get to see my sister if it wasn't for your help."

As William got nearer to home, he could hear loud voices farther up the street, which was unusual for that time of night. Mr Cooper stopped William. "Stay where you are for a minute, son."

"Why? What's wrong, Mr Cooper? What's happened?"

"I'm not sure, William, except that there's been some trouble at your house. Constable Machin's up there now." Mr Cooper stretched out his arm in front of William as if to protect him. "Wait ... Stand still until they pass ... Here they come."

Constable Machin and another policeman William didn't recognise walked past, either side of a giant of a man whose hands were tied behind his back. Peter and Joseph were walking a couple of yards behind them.

Mr Cooper patted William on the back. "Right. Now off you go. Find out what's going on and see how you can help your mam and dad."

William went around to the back of the house and into the backyard, which was a real mess, and he picked up a battered top hat. In the kitchen, Dad was sat on a chair next to the table, and Mam was wiping his face with a flannel from a basin full of warm water. William knelt next to Dad, "What's happened? And who broke the window?"

"It's a long story, son. But let's just say your mam has probably saved my life."

William looked at Dad's face. He had a nasty cut all down his forehead and cheek. Ellen stopped her nursing duties for a moment. "Sit down now next to your dad, and he'll tell you all about it. I'll make some fresh tea."

William knelt next to John. "Shall I go fetch our Harry, Dad?"

"No, son. I don't think it's necessary to go all

the way to Leigh, and in any case, your mam's got enough on her hands as it is."

"Who broke the kitchen window, Dad?"

"In a minute, son. Ellen, have you got any fresh tobacco in the drawer?"

Dad must be feeling better. He took a few minutes filling his pipe with the fresh tobacco, and having lit his pipe, he blew clouds of smoke in William's face. Then they both had the usual fit of coughing. "Well, it's like this. Peter took young Joseph to Wigan, and they went to the Shovel and Broom on the Manchester Road. Although he should really be mixing with lads his own age, apparently Peter got involved in a game of cards with a rough gang of Irishmen at least ten years older."

William leaned in towards his Dad, eager to know what happened next.

"There's this right bad lot. Paddy Doyle's his name—well over six feet tall and built like a brick privy, long white hair and no teeth, and always wears a black top hat like an undertaker. I'm not sure what happened, but suddenly Doyle turned over the table and screamed he was going to murder Peter. Anyway, both boys ran for their lives and, in half an hour, covered over three miles back here."

Mam handed Dad and William a mug of tea each.

"They were both frightened to death by the look of them, as well as being out of breath from running all that way." Dad nodded and had another fit of coughing. "Peter had stupidly told them that he and his brother were in lodgings in Stanley Road. He was sure that Doyle wasn't far behind, as by the time they were knocking on the front door here, there was some kind of commotion at the bottom of the road, and Doyle could clearly be heard shouting, 'Where? Up there?'"

"What had Peter done then, Dad?"

"I've no idea, son. But Doyle was probably off his head and just looking for a fight. I'm not surprised, as Paul Machin told me he's well known around the Wigan area. It was only last month that he was released from Lancaster after doing ten years for manslaughter. I'm surprised he hasn't been shipped off to the colonies before now. Not the sort decent folk should be mixing with."

"From the state of the backyard and the broken window, he must have been here. And I picked up the hat on my way in."

"Oh yes. He was here all right and left his mark too. I told the boys to stay in their room and then went out of the front door and onto the street. No sooner had I stepped out into the street than the hens and pigeons raised the alarm, making one hell of a racket, followed by the kitchen window being smashed. I dashed down the side of the house and ran straight into Doyle, who hit me across the face with a big wooden club, knocking me to the ground. I'm sure he would have killed me if it hadn't been for your mam."

"Bigger they come, harder they fall, my old dad used to say. So I hit him over the head with the garden spade."

"So you did, Mam. She hit him so hard William, knocked him out cold. Then just as he was coming to, Maggie arrived back with the police."

"I saw Constable Machin and the other constable with the big man. I take it must have been Doyle. Peter and Joseph were with them. They've caused a lot of trouble tonight, Dad. What can you do now?"

"I'm not going to have your mam put in danger son. So they'll have to find new lodgings somewhere else tomorrow. I think Mrs Cooper might well take them on. You had better get yourself off to bed now. We'll be going up shortly."

William got up from the table ready to go upstairs, while his mam was rummaging in the pocket of her apron. "Your brother was here earlier and left this for you." She gave William an envelope with his name on it. He'd never had a letter before.

Dad smiled and winked. "Go on then son, and open it."

William sat down again and opened the envelope. It was a handwritten note, not long:

Dear Brother William,

I am getting married to Leah on 28 June. And as you've always been my best friend, I want you to be my best man.

Harry.

William jumped up from the table holding his letter. Mam and Dad had never seen him so happy. "Best man! What do I have to do, Dad?"

"Not a lot. You will have to wear a jacket and tie and make sure Harry gets to the church on time. After the service, everyone will be going back to the Ivy for a drink and sandwiches, so that will be another first for you, going to the pub." Dad smiled and winked for the second time in five minutes.

Mam, meanwhile, was enjoying every moment of William's excitement on being asked to be Harry's best man and the thought of Harry getting married.

"At the reception in the Ivy, the other thing you must do, William, is to give a speech. The best man always says a few words."

"A speech, Mam? What will I say?"

"Well, I suppose just what Harry said in his letter—that he's always been your best friend and that, when you were small, he taught you all about playing football."

The *Wigan Observer* of 5 July 1892 carried a report, and William couldn't wait to get his hands on the paper that evening before Dad had quite finished his meal. This was the first time William had seen his name in print:

> Last Friday, 28 June 1892, Mr Henry Gregory (known as Harry) was married to Leah Welsby at the Parish Church Leigh, St Mary the Virgin. The bride was given away by her father, Mr David Welsby, and the best man was the groom's brother Mr William Gregory, aged 13. The happy couple will live at 5 Owens Yard in Stanley Road, Aspull.

CHAPTER 2

Opportunity Knocks

WILLIAM HAD TAKEN over as Dad's drawer two weeks after Harry's wedding eight years ago, and at the same time, Harry had taken charge of his own coalface.

Now with Leah and four children to support, he was working every shift possible, provided of course that he could get his own thrutcher and drawer to do the same. If they were unable to, William and Jimmy Makinson would often make up the team.

For the past six months, William had been seeing a lot of Elizabeth Cubbin, Leah's regular babysitter. Last week he'd introduced her to the rest of the Gregory family for the first time, after which everyone referred to her as William's lady friend. However, instead of meeting Elizabeth as usual, this evening he had gone to the Ivy for a pint with Harry after work before going home for dinner.

When he closed the back door behind him, Mam and Dad were, as always, sat in their rocking chairs either side of the fire Mam knitting for Harry's children and Dad enjoying his pipe while reading this week's *Wigan Observer*.

"Your dinner's in the oven William."

"Thanks, Mam. Best cook in the world you are."

"It's nice to be appreciated son. Do you think Elizabeth is a good cook then?"

"I think so, if she takes after her mam. Also, with Mr Cubbin owning the only grocery shop this side of Wigan, there's never a shortage of food in their house."

Dad said nothing, just smiled, drew deeply on his pipe, and continued studying his paper. Then, looking up, he pointed his pipe towards Ellen, "Interesting. In the letters page here, love, the Canadian government agency in Liverpool has written to the editor calling for experienced miners to emigrate to Canada."

Ellen looked up from her sewing. "Why on earth would you want to go to Canada at your time of life?"

John chuckled loudly. "No, not me, my love. But maybe thirty years ago I might have considered it. Seriously, though, I bet it may appeal to some younger ones around here." He glanced sideways towards William at the table. He opened the paper again and read, "It says here, in Glace Bay, Nova Scotia, the Dominion Coal Company has an urgent need for an additional twelve to fifteen hundred extra workers, of which at least five hundred must be experienced miners. Housing would be available at a low rent, and the wages are double the rates here in Lancashire. You are about the right age now at twenty-one, William. If anything comes of your romance with your lady friend —what's her name?— it might be worth considering."

Ellen put her sewing on the kitchen table, took the kettle from the fire, and filled the teapot for fresh tea. "By lady friend, I take it you mean Elizabeth John?"

"Yes, very nice girl you have there, William. I remember her mam from school. You could do much worse, you know."

William didn't say a word. He felt quite embarrassed talking about Elizabeth. He took his plate to the kitchen sink and then pulled up his chair nearer to Dad, who handed him the paper. "I already heard about this Canada letter, Dad. Jimmy Makinson told me. He's always talking about a better life outside of Lancashire, and it sounds to me as though he might well be interested in going." William took the paper back to the table and spent five minutes reading the letters page, in particular the piece about Canada. It all sounded very exciting. He sat deep in thought for a while and then gave the paper back to Dad and went upstairs to wash and change.

John picked up the *Observer* again where he'd left it and turned to the sports reports on the back page. "You know, Ellen, I always think of Saturday evenings as my favourite night of the week, just the two of us here."

"Yes, and mine too, John. It is nice and quiet, and our William will probably go out later. Is there anything else in the paper this week?" Ellen loved listening to him reading from the paper on Saturday evening.

"Well, my love. According to this piece on the front page, after the riots in Blackburn and Burnley earlier this year, the police arrested three Irishmen from Wigan who set fire to Ainsworth's Mill in Darwen. Last week, they were each sentenced at the Manchester Assizes to eight years in Strangeways; that's the new prison, you know."

"And so they should have been put away. It's lucky there was no one killed."

John nodded and puffed hard on his pipe, remembering how violent the riots had been. "I do understand how it all came about, but then everyone lost in the end. If you burn down the mill, the owners lose their fat profits, while the workers' means of making a living also goes up in smoke."

Nearly another hour passed in silence, both deep in their own thoughts. Then John folded the paper, tapped his pipe ash into the fire, and fumbled in his pocket for his tobacco. "I saw Bea at the Finger Post this morning on my way home from work. It was pouring with rain, and she was in the shelter with all the children. I don't know how she manages on her own."

Ellen nodded in agreement. "She's coped very well since losing Edwin in the accident—what with four children and taking in washing as well. Thank goodness these days there's schooling for her first two."

John relit his pipe, which, as usual, caused Ellen a fit of coughing.

Then she continued, "How old do you reckon she is then?"

"Who? Bea, you mean?"

Ellen smiled but didn't look up from the material she was cutting. John took in several deep puffs on his pipe, staring into the fire and picturing seeing Bea and the children earlier in the day. Then having made up his mind, he waved his pipe towards Ellen, "Fifty, Fifty-five-ish, going on, I'd say. Maybe a little bit younger?"

This confirmed to Ellen that he wasn't very good at judging ages. Her smile grew even broader, and she shook her head. "Well, she's actually twenty-seven—five years younger than me. When she was ten, she started working underground as her dad's thrutcher. She married Edwin at seventeen and has since had the children. I agree she does look older, but then, don't we all?"

In John's mind, Ellen hadn't changed since the day they were married. At barely five feet tall, she was still very trim, despite having had nine children, and was always neatly dressed with her dark-brown hair brushed back in a bun. "You see, love, to me you're still the same girl I met at your cousin Joan's wedding all those years ago. You haven't changed at all."

Ellen turned her eyes back to her knitting, quite embarrassed at the unexpected compliment.

"Perhaps it might have been different for you if you'd been at the pit like Bea instead of being at home nursing your dad. I know that must have been hard work. But in the long run, it was probably better for you than working on the pit brow."

"That's true, John. I hadn't thought of it quite like that before. Just imagine, if the Education Act hadn't been passed, our Alice could well have been working on the pit brow or at Dicconson's Mill for at least the past twelve months."

John took his watch from his waistcoat pocket. "Come on then, love. It's gone eleven, and we should be getting some sleep. I think our William's having an early night."

Ellen stood and lit the candle on the sideboard. "Yes, we should. It's been a long day, and I have lots to do tomorrow after we've been to the chapel. It looks as though our William's fallen asleep on the bed. He won't be going anywhere tonight."

Upstairs, they were undressing ready for bed, and John was sat on the chair pulling his boots off, when suddenly Ellen put her fingers to her mouth. "Sssshh. John, did you hear that? Sounds like the siren."

John rested his feet and listened carefully, but he couldn't hear anything. "No. Can't be, love, and not at midnight on a Saturday. There are only the safety men at the pit at this time."

Ellen cupped her hand to her ear. "No. There it is again."

"Yes, I can hear that now," said John. "But that's

not the pit siren, Ellen. The only other place I can think of is the Albion Foundry. I'd better get dressed and have a look. They don't sound the alarm without something happening you know."

Another hour passed before John returned home. Ellen had dressed, added more coal to the fire, and put the kettle on to boil. They sat at the kitchen table drinking tea. "Thanks, Ellen. Just what I needed. Damned chilly out there now."

"Well?" asked Ellen.

"Yes. Sure enough, it was a fire at the foundry. I thought I hadn't heard that alarm before. Thank God there was only the maintenance crew working, same as at the pit."

"Anyone hurt John?"

"It was all in hand by the time I got there. Spoke to Dr Walker, and he told me that two men were killed when a build-up of gas caused an explosion. A third was taken to the infirmary badly burned. No names yet, but whoever it is, some poor families will hear some rotten news before dawn I'd say."

"Yes, John. We're well used to accidents around here, and there seems to be no way of avoiding them. But it's more often than not the pit I think of, John. Anyway, no matter where, and whether it's someone badly hurt or sadly dies, my prayers are with them and their families tonight."

Love Is in the Air

It was the first shift back at the pit after the three-day Christmas break. Usually it had been just two, but this year they had been given the option of taking Christmas Eve day off, unpaid of course.

George Marsden, William's thrutcher, hadn't turned in for work this morning as his mam had been taken to the hospital late last night. The banksman sent down a foreign worker with an unpronounceable name in his place. Jimmy was filling in as drawer just for this shift. "No idea where this one comes from or what his name is. Let's call him Jack, shall we, William?"

"Sounds good enough to me, Jimmy. So let's just see how we get on then."

They had only been working for about half an hour when "Jack" crawled up behind William and tapped him on the shoulder. "Mr, come." He beckoned.

So William backed out to see what the problem was.

Jimmy was sat with his back to the wall grinning from ear to ear. "I'm sorry, William. I just lost my temper and clipped him round the ear. This isn't

24

working. He's positively dangerous. Hasn't got a clue."

"How much is in the tub so far, Jimmy?"

"Less than half full, I'd say," Jimmy replied.

"Okay, Jimmy. Let's call it a day. Come on then, Jack give me a hand to move the tub to one side, and the next shift can take over. That's cost us the wages for today." Jimmy took 'Jack' by the arm and showed him how to push the tub to one side. And then they both gave it one great shove, and it came off the rail, trapping William against the wall.

"Are you hurt, William?"

"Twisted my ankle I think, Jimmy."

"So you don't think anything's broken, William?"

"No. I don't think so. But whatever, it hurts like hell, Jimmy."

"We'll get you back up top as quick as we can and get it checked out. Come on, Jack. You're going to have to help me with him now."

William wrapped an arm around each of their shoulders, and they slowly made it back to the cage. At the medical centre, the orderly looked at William's ankle. "I'm pretty sure nothing's broken, William. But you're going to have some pretty bad bruising, I'd say. Just to be on the safe side, though, I'll see if Dr Walker's free to have a look. He was still here half an hour ago."

The doctor saw William about ten minutes later and confirmed that nothing was broken but that he should rest for a few days to allow the bruising time to heal before returning to work.

Elizabeth came to see William at home every evening, and they would spend an hour chatting in the front room. This was the first time they had spent much time together by themselves.

After a couple of days, they began talking about the future as though assuming they would be together. "But what do you think about possibly moving to live in Canada? Jimmy and Peter Spellman seem pretty keen on the idea, and I thought that life would be much better over there from the sound of it."

Elizabeth's answer took William by surprise. "I'd go with you if that's what you wanted."

"You mean as a couple, Elizabeth? Get married, do you mean?"

"Yes. Of course, if that's what you want. I know my mam thinks we're a good match, and I'm sure Dad likes you."

William took Elizabeth's hand, and they kissed. "I'll speak to your dad tomorrow."

The following morning, William was up extra

early to go over to Leigh and catch Mr Cubbin before he left to open the shop. Half an hour later, he was approaching Wigan Road.

He spotted Sid Morley on the opposite side of the street. They had both been in the same class at school. While William had followed his dad working at the pit, Sid was now a fireman covering both Leigh and Aspull. He waved over. "You're out early today, William. And what brings you this way?"

"Seeing Mr Cubbin hopefully before he leaves for the shop. Then off to work myself later. Anyway, how're you keeping, Sid?"

"Doing just fine now, thanks. Have you heard the news?"

"What news would that be then?"

"I've just come off night shift, and the banksman told me that Queen Victoria died yesterday at the place on the Isle of Wight."

"That is sad news. She seems to have been there forever. Good age, wouldn't you say?"

"Yes, eighty-two, my mam reckons. Dad says she must have been on the throne over sixty odd years or more."

"My mam won't know yet. Very loyal supporter of the royal family, my mam, so she'll be quite upset when she hears. Anyway, I've got to dash now, Sid. Be seeing you sometime."

Number 81 was only a little farther up the street, and William was only just in time to catch Mr Cubbin, who was on the doorstep about to leave as he arrived. Another moment chatting to Sid, and he would have been too late. "Hello, William. Can't stop now, I'm sure I know why you're here, and you both have my blessing. Mrs Cubbin, and I couldn't have wished for a better match for our Elizabeth. Good luck!" He shook William's hand and slapped him on the back, and then he was gone.

And so 22 January 1901 would forever be a date he would never forget. It was the day on which Mr Cubbin agreed to his marrying Elizabeth, as well as the date of Queen Victoria's death.

It took another two and a half years before they had saved enough to get married, as well as allowing sufficient time for Elizabeth and her mother to come to terms with the sudden death of John Cubbin from a heart attack soon after Christmas 1902.

William and Elizabeth were eventually married at the Parish Church, West Leigh, on 10 October 1903, and they lived in Wigan Road with Mrs Cubbin. Baby Ellen was born a year later followed by a son, John, in August 1905.

Although Mrs Cubbin didn't have a regular income, she did have some money left over from the sale of the shop. Nevertheless, with a wife and two children to support, William was finding it difficult to cope financially, to say the least. So, after much debate on all sides of the family, they were eventually all agreed that he should explore the possibility of emigrating to Canada, provided there was still a demand for additional immigrant mineworkers from Europe on similar terms as had been advertised some five years previously.

William wrote a letter to the Canadian agency in Liverpool. He received a reply a week later confirming that the demand was probably now more urgent than ever, that the terms were much the same as in 1900, and that the wages had been increased significantly in recent years. Provided that William attended an interview locally and that he was certified fit by a doctor, he was accepted just before Christmas with a forecast leaving date sometime the following summer, sailing from Liverpool.

CHAPTER 3

A Cruel Twist of Fate

ON SATURDAY MORNINGS the Gregory household was quiet, other than occasionally when Bea called in to see Ellen for a chat and a cup of tea. Today, John was working the morning shift, while William and Harry had gone to the Bolton versus Blackburn Rovers match instead. Ellen found this quite funny as she told Bea, "You would think it would be the other way round—sons at work while the father takes the day off at the football? After all, both boys are now married with children to support. And what with William emigrating to Canada in July, it's even more important that he's at work and earning money."

"Of course, I see what you mean Ellen. They should be at work. But on the other hand I suppose they're spending as much time together as is possible before William goes off. They've always been so close, and there won't be many more chances between now and July."

The Saturday routine was always the same for Ellen—the early morning feed for the chickens and pigeons; black leading the kitchen range and relaying the fire; preparing the hotpot ready for cooking; laying out John's clean clothes on the bed; and, finally, by midday, having the tin bath and towels ready in front of the kitchen fire.

John arrived home a little after one o'clock, and when he had finished his bath, he wrapped a towel around his middle, went upstairs, and fell fast asleep on the bed. It was gone four o'clock when he woke. He rinsed his face, dressed, and went down to the kitchen. Ellen was busy putting out a large bowl of lamb hotpot and a doorstop slice of bread for John. This was his favourite meal of the whole week. It still seemed odd now that, most times, there were only the two of them to share what had always in the past been the only time when all the family got together. Tomorrow would be different, when at least Nellie and Bertha would be at home for dinner.

They sat opposite each other to eat, and as John rarely spoke when he was eating, they would normally exchange their news afterwards. In no more than five minutes, John had finished the hotpot and then wiped the inside of his bowl clean with the last piece of bread. The satisfied smile on his face showed his appreciation. "I would swear Ellen, that's the best hotpot I can remember."

Ellen laughed as she cleared the empty bowls and bread plates from the table and took them to the stone sink. "But you said that last Saturday John. In fact, you say the same every Saturday. The rest of the lamb joint is for tomorrow, sliced with prayters and cabbage (see "Terminology"). She was still smiling to herself as she poured a kettle of boiling water into the sink to wash the dishes. The stone sink was the latest addition to the kitchen and had only been built in a month ago, together with the tap, which was their first indoor running water.

John got up from the table and settled into his rocking chair by the fire to read this week's *Observer*. Ellen washed up the supper things and then made herself comfortable opposite John and took up her knitting. John looked over the top of the paper and smiled at Ellen, "I heard some news today about this business in Canada."

Ellen leaned forward, eager to know what this news was. "Yes? What was that then John?"

"I heard that the Makinson lad and young Peter Spellman had applied to go. They must have been talking to our William. I'm sure Edward would have said something. He used to see a lot of Peter but not so much these days since they work different shifts. Of course, if they all went at the same time, at least William wouldn't be on his own."

It was after six o'clock by the time John finished his after-dinner pipe and had read every page in the paper. Ellen chatted about the local gossip she'd heard from Bea earlier in the day, most of which didn't make much sense to John, as it largely involved children he didn't even know.

As the clock struck seven, John took his jacket off the hook on the back door and put his cap on. "You know what love? It's a nice evening out, so if you don't mind, I think I'll take a stroll down to the Finger Post to see Chris for an hour."

Ellen was now busy with her knitting. The broad smile of earlier returned as she nodded in agreement. "No. You go off love. You've had a hard week. Remember me to Chris now."

Just as John always repeated the same compliment about her hotpot every Saturday, at the same time each week, it came as no surprise to Ellen that he would also go to see Chris. And it really didn't seem to matter whether or not the weather outside was fine, because even if it was pouring with rain or snowing, he would still go.

John Gregory and Chris Fielding had been the best of friends since they were children. Having been badly injured in an accident ten years ago, Chris had given up working underground at the pit and, since then, had been selling beer at weekends to a group of drinking pals in the front room of his home opposite the Finger Post. John generally went for a beer with Chris on Saturday evening and occasionally on Sunday as well.

Other regular drinkers at Number 7 each had his own reasons for avoiding being seen drinking in Aspull. James Harding JP, as a local magistrate would have to pass judgement on those miscreants who drank too much and became involved in fighting with drinkers visiting from Wigan; Dr Walker would be called upon to tend to the injuries resulting from the all-too-frequent weekend altercations at the Ivy Inn, and in the case of the local constabulary, Sergeant Crawford and Constable Dent had responsibility for restoring peace and arresting the combatants once they had been patched up by the good doctor. Constable Alan Dent was a new arrival, having recently been transferred from the Sheffield Force after Paul Machin's retirement.

Magistrate James Harding would visit Chris either Saturday or Sunday, whenever he felt the urgent need to escape the clutches of the formidable Mrs Eliza Harding, if only for a couple of hours. For a time in the past, he had tried the garden shed. But that hadn't worked, for as long as she knew exactly where he was, there was to be no privacy. The only time in the past he found any peace of mind was when he was focussing on the cases before him in court—that is, until he discovered Chris Fielding's front room. There he was sure he wouldn't be found, and after a few glasses of Sumners extra strong dark ale, he would always return home in high spirits, which was at least good news for any unfortunates due to appear before the magistrates the following Monday morning. Dr Walker generally went to help him recover from often having to tend to the wounded in the lounge of the Ivy on Saturday night, often continuing into the early hours of Sunday morning.

The front room of Chris's home was quite large compared to most on Scot Lane. Furnished with a large oak dresser, a table, and four comfortable armchairs; it was usually dimly lit by a couple of candles in the evening, in addition to the dying embers in the fireplace. It was always warm and comfortable, the perfect retreat for gentleman drinkers escaping from—well, whatever it was they were escaping from.

It was about half past seven by the time John got to the Finger Post and knocked on Chris's front door. "Ah, John. Good to see you. Come on in. How have you been keeping? It's a full house this evening. Mr Harding and Doctor Walker are here. And the new Constable Alan Dent was in earlier but didn't get to finish his first beer before Sergeant Crawford arrived and hauled him off somewhere. Must have been something important."

John followed Chris into the front room. James Harding was sat in an armchair with his long legs outstretched. He was holding a half-empty glass of dark ale and was quietly puffing on his briar—a picture of utter contentment. Chris did the introductions. "You know John Gregory?"

James stood and shook John's hand. "Yes, of course. How are you? And Mrs Gregory is keeping well I hope?"

"Fine thanks," John replied. "And Mrs Harding too?"

John's enquiry went unanswered.

Dr Walker smiled and waved. "Twice in the same week John."

Chris pointed John towards the remaining empty

armchair. "Why? Is everything all right at home, John?"

"Yes all's well, thanks, Chris. The doctor called on Wednesday just to leave a certificate for William before he goes to Canada."

"I got a delivery of a new dark ale this morning from Sumners. Fit to blow your head off according to Henry Rawcliffe. Here, try a glass on me. We've already had a couple."

John took a sip from his glass and then fumbled in his pocket for his pipe and tobacco. Then all four lit their pipes at more or less the same time. Other than a fit of coughing from each, quiet descended on the room for the next five or so minutes.

Then Chris pointed his pipe towards John, "What's that again you have there, John? It's a fine strong-smelling tobacco. Very nice I always think."

"Gawith's number four, Chris. Always smoked it—well at least since I was fifteen."

When all four were seated, the difference in height wasn't so noticeable. Chris and John were no taller than five feet five and of stocky build, and Doctor Walker wasn't much taller; Magistrate Harding, on the other hand was very tall and thin with a prominent nose—it wouldn't be the first time someone had commented that his appearance put a different slant on the expression 'up before the beak'! (See "Terminology".)

What most folks in Aspull thought looked odd was when Mrs Harding officiated at the opening of the annual hospital summer fete and, at barely five feet tall, stood next to her husband, who stood well over six feet; odd seemed something of an understatement. Nonetheless, despite being short, Mrs Harding always appeared very confident. She maintained an air of aloofness; never smiled; and, when introduced to anyone, always adopted a look of distaste. Mrs Eliza Harding was definitely not from Lancashire.

While Chris was refilling everyone's glass, John's mind mulled over what had been said earlier. "I wonder what on earth happened to need such urgent attention from Alan and Sergeant Crawford?"

"I'm sure we'll find out soon enough," said James. "You know, I once heard it said that nothing much happens in Aspull. But it just shows you how quickly people forget." He sat back in the chair again and relit his pipe. "Bearing in mind that in the past three years alone, we first of all had the nasty business of the youths from Wigan who beat poor Constable Pollard senseless in the street; then old Seddon murdered his missus. I don't think that counts as not much happening, don't you think? As a magistrate, of course, I see it all."

"Quiet little village eh?" Chris looked at the others in turn, confirming they were all of like mind. They all sat quietly for a moment, deep in thought as they recalled the Seddon murder and when the constable had been beaten up for no apparent reason. The whole village had been shocked at the time.

"I knew the Seddon family from the chapel," said John. "She wasn't exactly what you would call a pleasant woman, although I wouldn't have gone so far as strangling her to death. She probably didn't know about you selling beer, Chris, what with her being a leading light in the Wigan Band of Hope. I suppose if she'd known, she might have wanted to do you in. Instead, her old man got her first. So at least you owe him a debt of gratitude there."

James smiled and nodded. Mrs Seddon had been a friend of his wife's. He was relishing this conversation. "I see what you mean, John. But murder is murder, and there's never a good ending to it. I've seen a few in my time over the past twenty odd years. When you hear the full story in court, I'm not at all surprised it doesn't happen more often. I had to go up to Lancaster when Seddon was hanged."

Chris and the doctor both smiled and nodded,

remembering the nasty business. John said nothing, but he wondered whether James had ever thought of getting rid of Mrs Harding. If anyone could get away with murder, surely none better than a magistrate?

Chris got up from the table and poured more beer all round. The new ale was going down well. "Whatever's happened, they had to call the inspector from Wigan on his horse. I suppose that's a question of good news or bad, you might say. The good news is for folk with an allotment; horse muck is damned good stuff for the soil. But seriously, I hope it's not bad news."

"So do I," said James. "I mean, I hope it's not bad news. Although I believe it's true what they say about horse muck." Now in full flow, he continued, "Reminds me of the business with the two from up Holly Nook, fighting over the horse muck left by the coal delivery wagon. The driver got down to sort them out, and then they both set about him, and he ended up in the infirmary. Crawford hauled them off to the station, and they were up before me the following Monday."

John chuckled. "Yes. I know them both. I think you gave them both a fine of five shillings each."

"I did," James replied. "But apart from the serious

injury to the driver, I did find it quite amusing at the time."

For the next hour the subject changed, and they discussed Bolton Wanderers' matches through to the end of the season, especially of interest since James had recently been appointed a director.

The new ale went down a treat, and John must have had four or five glasses, which was much more than he usually had. He checked the time on his pocket watch. "A quarter past ten already!" He got up to leave and could certainly feel the effects of the ale. "Much as I like your company gentlemen, and the ale of course, I really have to go now. How much do I owe you, Chris?"

"A shilling will do fine John. Anyway, it's been good to see you."

John paid Chris, shook hands with the magistrate and Dr Walker, and then saw himself out the front door and back on to Scot Lane.

The walk back home up Stanley Road gave him plenty of time to clear his head. As always, Ellen had been right. And despite the chilly feel in the night air, John felt on top of the world after a few beers.

It was a particularly dark night, and with no street lighting, it was difficult to see very far ahead. As John approached the house, he was surprised to see a bicycle he recognised as Constable Dent's propped up against the lower step. Curious, he quickened his step, and when he opened the back door into the kitchen, he sensed that something was badly wrong. The room was silent. Ellen was sat in the rocking chair staring into the fire. William was sat at the table with his head cradled in his arms. And Alan Dent stood resting his back against the sink. Their silence painted a very sombre picture.

"What's to do, Alan?" John asked.

The look on Alan's face confirmed that indeed something really serious had happened. He said nothing.

"Trouble at t' Mill then? What is it?' (See "Terminology".)

Alan put his arm around John's shoulder. "I'm sorry, John. There's no easy way to say this, but there's been a terrible accident, and Harry's dead."

John froze. It felt as though someone had stabbed him to the heart. He felt quite faint and sank into the chair opposite Ellen. He leaned forward and reached for her hand, at the same time shaking his head in disbelief. John had always been the strong one when it came to coping with any major family issue, but now Ellen could only see a look of despair on his face, and just a hint of a tear in the corner of his eye. "No. It can't be. Not our Harry. This just doesn't happen to one of your own." He turned towards William, "What … what happened, William? Where … where's Leah?"

William looked to his dad. "I don't know everything yet, but it was an accident. Happened at the Ivy Hotel. Jimmy Simm was with him. Leah and the children are with Elizabeth."

Constable Dent drained his tea and put his helmet on. "I'd best be off and leave you good folk to it. But if there's anything I can do, John, Ellen, you know where we are."

John had been indoors about half an hour when Maggie arrived. She and Elizabeth had gone straight down to Leah as soon as they'd heard the news about Harry, so that she would know much more about what had happened.

William stood and put his cap on. "Now you're here, Maggie, I'd better go and see how they're getting on. See if there's anything I can do."

"They were all right when we left," said Maggie.

William kissed his mam's forehead, shook hands with his dad, and then closed the kitchen door behind him.

Maggie poured herself a cup of tea and pulled up

a chair next to Ellen, "With all this going on, how's little Billy been, Mam?" she asked.

Ellen spoke for the first time. "He's been as good as gold. Slept most of the day. God bless him, he's no trouble at all."

After Maggie had finished her tea, she went through to the front room, where Ellen had put Billy to sleep wrapped in a blanket in a drawer from the sideboard.

Now on their own, very little passed between John and Ellen for the next hour while they sat quietly thinking about poor Harry and what on earth would become of Leah and the children.

John broke the silence, "Furthest thing from my mind, this. Our Harry of all people. And with Leah and the children, what's to do, I ask myself? And with our William going off to Canada in July, Elizabeth will have enough on her hands with her own.

Ellen stood and re-filled the kettle to make fresh tea, and as she turned from the fire she kissed John gently on the forehead before sitting down opposite him. "William's obviously taking this very hard; the two of them have been inseparable since he was born. As for us, we'll make do somehow, as we always do. Let's just pray for poor Leah and the children. I can't imagine how they must be feeling right now."

John nodded in agreement and then looked at the clock on the mantelpiece. "It's nearly one o'clock in the morning. Yes, we should try to get some rest now. It'll be a busy day tomorrow."

RIP, Harry

Harry's funeral took place at St Elizabeth's on Wednesday 14 February. And as so often was the case on these occasions, the weather was overcast and cold, and it rained on and off all day. The service was conducted by the Reverend James, and the church was mainly filled with retired folk or young mothers with children. The coffin was carried in by William, Jimmy Simm, and four of Harry's old school friends.

The pathetic sight of Leah and the seven children as they entered the church was something everyone present would never forget, and the Reverend James's closing remarks were brief. "We have all gathered here today to remember Harry, who brought so much happiness into all our lives and was so cruelly taken from us far too soon. We do not mourn and feel sadness for ourselves, but we are comforted in the knowledge that he is now resting at peace."

"Amen," everyone responded.

The *Observer*, a week later, carried a report about Harry. John couldn't bear to read it, so he asked William.

"Mam, Dad. It's on page four."

It read:

A collier named as Henry (Harry) Gregory (32) met his death on Saturday, 10 February 1906, when, along with another man, he went into the Ivy Hotel in Aspull and had three glasses of ale. Subsequently, as they were about to leave, Gregory said he would go out the back. He was not seen alive again.

A few minutes later, the landlord went down to the cellar, where he found Henry lying at the foot of the steps, his head being on the floor and his foot on the bottom step. He had a large wound on the back of his head and, on being carried upstairs, was found to be dead.

An Inquest was held at the Ivy Hotel on Monday, 12 February, when evidence was heard by Mr Butcher, the coroner for Bolton District. The jury returned a

verdict of accidental death. Mr Gregory of
3 Cleveleys Yard Aspull leaves a widow,
Leah Gregory, and seven children.

Memories from the past came flooding back—
first losing baby Peter, now Harry; Ellen left the
table and sat by the fire opposite John. It had all
been too much, and suddenly her previous composure
melted away. She held her hands over her eyes and
sobbed, heartbroken. All those years ago, it had been
bad enough losing baby Peter. But now Harry—the
burden of grief would bear heavily on her heart for
the rest of her days.

CHAPTER 4

Farewell Aspull

IT WAS JUST before eight o'clock on Monday morning, 23 July, when John opened the front door to William and Elizabeth. "You're both out early this morning. Come on in. Go through to the kitchen. The kettle's just about boiling. Your mam will be back downstairs shortly."

They followed him through to the kitchen, and Elizabeth immediately busied herself putting out the teacups on the table.

"Well, Dad, it looks like there's not going to be much time this morning after saying cheerio to everyone. Ernie's picking me up at ten o'clock to take me to the station. It was a good idea of yours to see everyone here. I'm sure one of the girls will walk Elizabeth back down home later after I've gone, and I thought maybe our Bertha would stay with her for a while and help with the children."

Ellen came downstairs. She kissed Elizabeth on the cheek, and they hugged each other. She then gave Elizabeth the brown paper parcel from the table. "Well. It's the big day today, Elizabeth. I want you to make sure that William takes this with him. I know it's the middle of summer here, but he's going to need this come the winter in Canada."

"Thanks, Ellen. But what is it?"

"It's Dad's woollen overcoat. He never wears it these days."

"That's very kind of you, Ellen. But are you sure?"

"Yes. Of course, I'm sure. Dad read somewhere that it gets bitterly cold out there in the winter." Elizabeth passed the parcel to William. "That will do you nicely come winter, don't you think, love?"

"Yes, it will. Just what I needed." William knew that his dad did wear the coat when it was cold. It was so sad that having worked so hard and sacrificed so much over the years, his parents still wanted to give everything even now. It was a struggle to hold back the tears. "Thanks, Dad, but only if you're certain you're not going to need it next winter."

John smiled and winked at William but said nothing.

Ellen put a reassuring hand on Elizabeth's shoulder. "It's the least we can do. And you mustn't worry, Elizabeth, while our William is gone. We'll look after you. How's your mam, by the way?"

"Thanks, Ellen," Elizabeth replied. "It's very comforting to know you're all here, especially as Mother isn't too good at the moment."

For the next hour or so, there seemed to be a constant stream of family and friends arriving to see William before he left for Wigan Station and, from there, the train to Liverpool. Surprisingly, even Edward came over from Blackrod, and it must have been well over a year since he had last been seen by anyone in the family.

The importance of the occasion was noticeable by the fact that everyone turned up wearing his or her Sunday best clothes. The house was soon a hive of activity both indoors and out. Alice helped her mam, providing a never-ending supply of tea, while William and Elizabeth sat on the sofa in the front room and chatted to the visitors as they arrived. The backyard was also full of very excited children. For them, it was like a family party, whilst at the same time viewed with mixed feelings by the adults.

John wasn't at all keen on crowds of people in the house and took the children down to the allotment for a while. But after a little over an hour later, quite exhausted, he returned them all back up to the house.

Indoors, John put his head round the door of the front room and beckoned William. "Come on upstairs for a minute son. I have something I want to show you."

William followed his dad upstairs to the bedroom, wondering what the mystery was all about.

John opened the top drawer of the bedside cabinet and handed him his pocket watch, "Here. I want you to have it. Now that you have a good watch, you'll have no excuse for being late, so always allow yourself plenty of time."

"Dad. Are you sure? I don't know what to say." William stared at the watch and studied the engraving on the back. He knew how much it meant to his dad. It had been a gift from Ellen's father to John on the day of their wedding. The simple engraving read, "To John Gregory from Edward Fisher, October 1868."

William really couldn't find the words to thank his dad for giving him the watch. It was an item of such great sentimental value, and at the time, it was so unusual for the bride's father to make such a generous gift to the man about to marry his daughter. John was a man of few words. He simply

51

smiled and shook hands with his son—possibly for the last time, he thought.

William and Elizabeth were left alone in the front room for a few minutes to say their goodbyes. There were no words exchanged. Everything they had wanted to say had already been said. They just hugged and held each other very close. William kissed Elizabeth gently on the lips, while she bravely held back the tears. "Don't forget to write as often as you can and give me all the news. It'll be lonely out there until you arrive with the children."

Everyone had already left the house and gathered in the street outside. William and Elizabeth joined them just as Ernie arrived with the coal cart. He was the only one in working clothes, having just delivered a load to the Coopers.

Without prolonging the farewells, William climbed up next to Ernie. Turning back to wave goodbye to Elizabeth and the gathering of family and neighbours, he was close to tears himself. But he continued smiling and waving until they reached the bottom of Stanley Road. John and Ellen stayed indoors—too many goodbyes.

The Leaving of Liverpool

William had never been to Liverpool before, and after arriving at Lime Street Station, he asked at the ticket barrier for directions to the Docks and Harbour Board building.

"I'd say it's about a quarter of an hour's walk from here. Go out of the exit and turn right on the main street. If you keep straight on, you'll eventually come to the MDHB buildings on the right."

Nearly half an hour later, William stopped outside a large building with a sign, "Mersey Docks and Harbour Board" (MDHB). Inside, he joined the end of the long queue at the reception desk.

"William Gregory. Here's my letter from the Dominion Coal Company."

"Thanks, Mr Gregory. I've checked you in. By the way, you're all for the Dominion party today. Wait over there to your right, and you will be called shortly."

He didn't have long to wait before the same man from reception reappeared from behind the desk and called out through a megaphone, "Attention please. If you have registered for the Dominion Coal Company collect your belongings and follow me."

They were led outside into a yard and over to the

building opposite. There was a view of the docks to the left. "Over here is the accommodation block where you will be sleeping tonight. Mr Cameron, the ship's purser, will be along in a moment to show you around and explain the arrangements for the sailing tomorrow."

The thin, uniformed man turned and left them standing around with their bags and wondering what they were expected to do next.

"Fine carry on this is." William recognised the North Wales accent from the number of Welshmen working at the pit in more recent years. The man was short and wiry, wearing the biggest flat cap he could remember seeing before. *It's a wonder he can see anything from under that cap*, thought William.

"I'm sure there'll be a lot more hanging around before we get to Canada. I'm William Gregory by the way, from Aspull near Wigan."

They shook hands, "Ivor Griffiths, from Plas Power near Wrexham. How do?"

They didn't have to wait too long before another very stern-faced man in uniform appeared and showed them where they were to sleep.

"My name is Cameron, ship's purser, and when you need to speak to me, you will address me as Mr Cameron. Understood?"

They all muttered yes, acknowledging the instruction.

Mr Cameron continued. "Listen to me carefully. Tomorrow we will be sailing in the SS *Empress of Ireland*, and we are due to leave in the afternoon at 1530 hours. That is half past three. We are scheduled to be at sea for a total of twelve days, calling at Belfast; across the Atlantic, and then stopping at a number of ports in the United States; and, finally, on to Halifax, Nova Scotia, where you will all disembark."

The following day was fine and dry, and having got everyone together on board, the ship moved off from its mooring and just gone half past three. They were all crowded on deck as they passed the Liverpool Docklands. Then it seemed like no time at all before the *Empress* was heading for the open sea.

***

Destination Nova Scotia

As their last sight of England disappeared in the distance, the men remained standing at the rail, wondering whether they would see their families and friends again. William of course was comforted in the knowledge that arrangements were already in hand for Elizabeth and the children to join him in Canada once he was settled in Glace Bay.

After nearly an hour had passed since leaving Liverpool, one of the ship's crew came and called them to gather round him. "So that you know who I am, my name is Mr Shaw, and I am Mr Cameron's assistant purser on the *Empress of Ireland*. You have been allocated to Decks B and C below, where you will now take your belongings and find the bunk matching your tag number. Those whose surnames begin A to L will go to Deck B, and those whose names begin M to Z (and I know there are no Z's among you), go to Deck C."

William picked up his bags and started to follow the others towards the direction signs leading to the decks below.

"Wait! I haven't finished yet," Purser Shaw called out. "Now listen carefully to me. You can very easily get lost on board ship, so it's really important that you pay particular attention to all instructions. You will have noticed that you are now all on the port side, and for those who haven't sailed before, that is the left side of the ship. The port side is where all the Dominion Coal passengers must stay when up top, whereas the starboard side is reserved for our tourist class passengers, who are all accommodated on Deck A. The *Empress* is bound for Belfast, our first port of call, where we are scheduled to arrive in about three hours' time. Once the other passengers are on board in Belfast, you will again be addressed by the first officer in Mess Hall B/C. Are there any questions?'

Mr Shaw didn't wait for questions but turned and pointed. "The door over there signed B and C Decks leads to the stairs down to your accommodation. Now off you go."

William picked up his bags and waved to Ivor, "You must be next to me again Ivor. I'm B67."

"It's 68 I am, boyo. I'm with you."

Rather than three hours, it was nearer eight by the time they docked in Belfast Harbour. They waited another hour before Mr Shaw came back and led everyone to the mess hall, where they were addressed by the first officer. It was now nearly one o'clock in the morning.

"Welcome aboard the *Empress of Ireland*. I'm First Officer Charles MacKay. The delays we are currently experiencing are unavoidable and are beyond our control. It's now gone one, so I will be brief. There will be plenty of time to catch up on your rest in the coming days. The *Empress of Ireland* is a new ship, which has only been in service for the past six months. So I would ask that you bear this in mind and treat the ship, the crew, and all the facilities with respect. In return, we will make the next twelve days as comfortable for you as possible. Follow the advice given to you earlier by Mr Shaw, and also pay careful attention to any instruction issued by members of the ship's company during the crossing. We will be leaving Belfast mid-morning and crossing the Atlantic to the United States, where we are scheduled for a short stop in Philadelphia. Then our onwards journey takes us to Canada, where you will all disembark in Halifax, Nova Scotia. That's all for now, so return to your bunk areas and try to get some sleep."

The Atlantic crossing was uneventful, other than the weather, which was for the most part, raining heavily, with high winds and choppy seas. As a result, there was quite a lot of seasickness. Nevertheless, they quickly settled into a routine of eating, for those who felt like it and otherwise sleeping, playing cards, and writing letters home ready to post in Canada. And every evening, they entertained themselves with a singalong led by a tin miner from Cornwall who played the mouth organ.

On the first night, William and Ivor turned in to

their bunks at gone eleven, both still humming some of the tunes they recognised. "That was good, Ivor. Nice and jolly to cheer everyone up. Don't know what you thought. For me, some of the tunes sounded familiar but as for the words I hadn't a clue. Old Cornish folk songs I suppose."

The *Empress* had stopped for refuelling in Philadelphia in the early hours of the morning of 1 August, although William slept soundly throughout the operation. By the time he was awake, they were already back at sea and on the final leg of their journey.

It was three days later, after they had been fed at breakfast time, that Mr Shaw came to warn everyone to get ready for their arrival in Halifax. "We expect to arrive at about 1100 hours today, so that you now have about two hours to pack your belongings and assemble up top as you did when you first boarded. I will be checking your deck area below and expect to find you all present and correct on deck, not later than 1020 hours."

William and Ivor were, in fact, the first to vacate their bunk area and, once up on deck, had their first view of Canada and Halifax as they approached the harbour. "Looks very similar to Liverpool but on a smaller scale, wouldn't you say, Ivor?"

"Everywhere looks enormous to me William, compared with Plas Power. Now that's what I call small."

Compared with the past ten days, today it was unusually warm and sunny by the time the *Empress* was eventually secured dockside. This wasn't at all what William had expected, so wearing Dad's overcoat would obviously have to wait for another time later in the year. At half past five, they started down the gangway with their bags and on to the quayside, where they were met by a Dominion Coal representative wearing the now familiar uniform of dark grey trousers, navy jacket, and peaked cap.

"Call that a peaked cap Ivor. It's got nothing on the peak on yours."

"God bless my old mam, William. She said that at least I wouldn't be blinded by the sun. I don't know why she would think that, because the sun only shines in Plas Power twice a year."

They were soon organised into a rough line. After gathering up their baggage, they were led to the train waiting at the platform in the sidings, about two hundred yards away.

"Get yourselves onto the train and find a seat in the nearest open carriage; tea and sandwiches will be handed round as soon as we get underway. We are due to arrive in Sydney tomorrow evening, so make yourselves as comfortable as possible. It's a long journey. Any questions?"

William had missed Ivor in the crowd when they set off for the train. "Yes, sir. Where's Ivor Griffiths? We've travelled together since leaving Liverpool."

The officer checked his list of names, "Griffiths you say? I've no Griffiths on here. He must be with the other party due to leave on the following train."

William turned to the man now sat next to him. "Everything has been so well organised so far, and then without any warning, Ivor has now gone off to somewhere called Springhill. Come to think of it, he never did say where he was going once we'd arrived; I just assumed he was also going to Glace Bay."

In fact, William never heard anything of Ivor from that day on. As he was to learn in future years, no sooner would he get to know someone well, then the next minute they would be gone forever.

CHAPTER 5

New Beginnings

Cape Breton, Canada, 1906–1916

THE TRAIN JOURNEY was indeed a very long one, and when they eventually pulled into Sydney station, they had been travelling for over twenty-four hours. By this time, it was quite dark so they would have to wait for their first sight of their new home until the morning.

From the station, they were taken by bus to the single men's accommodation, close to the pit. William was so exhausted he didn't even bother to unpack any of his belongings but just took his boots off, rolled onto the straw-filled mattress, and was soon fast asleep, covered by the woollen blanket they'd been given.

At six o'clock the following morning, they were woken by a red-faced, smiley kind of man, who introduced himself. "I'm Dick Hepinstall, and as I'm now beyond the normal retirement age, I've been made responsible for looking after all newcomers to the pit. I hope you've all slept well. There's nothing much expected of you today except to clean up and get your meals in the canteen. Then you can spend some time exploring the area."

"Is there much to see then Mr Hepinstall?" a man at the other end of the room asked. He still sounded half-asleep.

"There is indeed. Glace Bay is a centre of industry, and the Dominion Coal Company is the major employer in the area. You will be working at the Hub Shaft, which is the largest pit in Glace Bay; the S & L Railway has its roundhouse and machine shop here. There's also a small port, which is the next most northern calling off point after Halifax for small ships; there's a thriving fishing community, as well as a busy boatbuilders' yard. But for me, the most important activity in Glace Bay, particularly in the winter season, is ice hockey. I've followed the Miners team since I arrived in Glace Bay. What you would probably not have known before you came out here is that Glace Bay is known as the birthplace of hockey. So, to answer your question, yes there is more than enough to keep you amused."

"Well, I'm gobsmacked. I never expected so much activity in such a small area."

Mr Hepinstall heard William's comments. "Gregory, isn't it?"

"Yes, sir."

"Well, I'm pleased to say that you're never going to be bored here. You should take your time to look around today. But don't leave the town area, as the black bears around these parts are always pretty hungry!"

Breakfast was in the canteen at seven o'clock. As William was waiting in the queue to be served, he felt a tug on his arm, and a familiar voice called, "Well, well. If it isn't William Gregory. We heard you were coming, didn't we, Pete?"

William turned, and much to his surprise, there, as large as life, stood Jimmy Makinson and Peter Spellman, grinning from ear to ear. "Jimmy! Pete! I hadn't expected to see you so soon. How are you both? How are things here?"

They all shook hands, comforted by having each other from Aspull to talk to.

Jimmy shook William's shoulder. "It's so good to see you again, William. We've only been here for the past two months. Just come off the night shift and on our way to breakfast. It takes a little while to settle in. But on the whole, life is pretty good here. What are you doing later?"

"Mr Hepinstall is taking us to see the pit later, but he warned us not to leave the immediate area surrounding the pit and accommodation because of the threat from bears. After that, I suppose I'm free."

Peter burst out laughing. "Dick always says that, Willum, to make sure you don't stray too far until you're more familiar with the area. In fact, bears are rarely seen anywhere other than the heavily forested areas and certainly nowhere near Sydney. Anyway, after breakfast when we've cleaned up and had a rest, then what about meeting at three o'clock outside J1?"

"I'll see you then," William replied.

After finishing his breakfast, William returned to J1 hut, where Mr Hepinstall was waiting to take the new arrivals group on a tour of the Hub Shaft pit yard and workings. "The pit was only sunk a little over forty years ago in 1861, so that you'll find that everything about the pit—the buildings, rail connections, and housing—are all relatively new compared with what you've been used to back home. After this short tour, you will at least know how to get to work."

At three, William was waiting for Jimmy and

Peter to appear. Sure enough, they turned up looking well rested after a few hours' sleep. "I thought we'd start by showing you around the town centre, William. It's probably the best place to start."

"That sounds good to me Jimmy. I believe most of the ones who arrived with me yesterday have gone off to the Miners' Social Club, although I didn't see it when Dick Hepinstall showed us round."

"I go in there most days for a game of cards," said Pete. It's just outside the pit yard. If we have time, we'll probably pop in there on our way back. What do you think, Jimmy?"

"Good idea Pete. I'm not so sure William is a card player, but it's as good a place as any until Elizabeth and the children come out. You'll also find it interesting if we're able to take a quick look around the dock area and, further along, where they moor the fishing boats."

"Thanks to you both for taking the time to show me around. I'll have lots to tell Elizabeth when I write home tonight."

Two tours into his first day and William was finding it all a bit overwhelming. But nevertheless, he was enjoying every moment. Although Sydney wasn't a big place compared with Wigan, he thought that the town was very similar, just on a smaller scale. "The shops will certainly supply all the basics when Elizabeth arrives," "I suppose so," both Jimmy and Pete echoed. Shopping was obviously not on their list of priorities.

With a couple of days to settle in and get used to the routine, William started working the day shift on the following Monday. He found that most things were much the same as at home. But two things stuck in his mind that first shift. First, there were two shafts, one for moving men underground in a metal-sided cage, as opposed to the platform arrangement back in Aspull, and the second shaft for moving coal tubs up and down. The other difference was that the full tubs were hauled from the front by ponies instead of boy drawers, although thrutchers were still used, making sure the tub wheels stayed on the rails. Just as important was their job clearing the muck left behind by the ponies, which they shovelled off the roadway onto the side. As a result, not only was it dark and damp underground, it also stunk to high heaven.

Through the first week, William worked alongside Hamish Campbell, who was an experienced miner at the hub. By end of the week, though, he hadn't learned anything new about the pit, other than the occasional snatches of conversation he was able to understand as Hamish had a very strong Scottish accent.

On Wednesday after work, William met Peter Spellman in the club. "I've been with Hamish Campbell this week, Pete. Do you know him?"

"Oh yes. Both Jimmy and I met him when we first arrived. Between the two of us, we couldn't make heads or tails of a word he said."

From the start of the second week, William was given his own face, supported by Niall Moore, who as thrutcher loaded the tubs, kept the pony's nosebag filled, and made sure there was enough water in the bucket to last for the whole shift.

On Sunday morning of his third week, William sat at a table in the club and wrote to Elizabeth:

> Dominion Hut 12
> Hub Shaft Pit
> Sydney,
> Glace Bay,
> Nova Scotia
>
> 19 August 1906
> Dear Elizabeth,
>
> I'm sorry that this is my first letter since arriving in Canada. But it's been so busy

from the moment we got off the train. There hasn't been a moment to spare.

We arrived at six o'clock in the evening of 5 August, and although daytimes at this time of year are still warm and sunny, when it gets to four, it comes in dark quickly and turns quite chilly.

The accommodation for single men is in a row of wooden huts with room for ten men in each. It's comfortable, and I'll be living here for the next twelve months until you come out. We get three meals a day in the canteen, and the food is good and plenty of it.

I met Jimmy Makinson, who you know, and Peter Spellman, who was a good friend of our Edward. They showed me around the town. I think you'll like it here, as it's got everything the same as Wigan, only smaller.

I've been at work now for three weeks, and the conditions are a little better than in Aspull. It looks like I'll be on permanent day shift. The others are on nights, so I will only see them on weekends. The pit is very modern compared to Aspull, and they have ponies underground to do much of the heavy work pulling the full coal tubs.

I'm thinking about you all every day and hope this finds you in good health and children behaving themselves.

With much love,

William x

PS. Meeting Jimmy and Peter later for a drink in the Miners' Social Club.

Reunion

Over three months had passed since William arrived in Sydney. Now in mid-November, the first snows had fallen, and it was bitterly cold, particularly at night. Now was the time he really appreciated having Dad's winter overcoat. The shops in Sydney sold lots of winter clothing which were quite expensive, so William had put off buying too much at the start, and managed to get by wearing thick woollen gloves, a fur hat, the overcoat, and two pairs of socks.

This week, he was on the day shift as usual, and on his way back across the pit yard, he called into the social club for a drink before the evening meal, which wouldn't be ready for another couple of hours. Wednesdays were usually very quiet. He chatted with the barman for about half an hour and then took his beer over to a corner table. There was a lot to think about before Elizabeth arrived with the children. Hopefully, they would be here soon after Christmas, so not long to go before they were together again. The lack of any news about family accommodation since he'd started work was never far from his mind. And until he heard more on the housing front, he couldn't even begin to think about what he might have to buy to get any new home fit for Elizabeth and the children to live in when they arrived.

William's thoughts were interrupted when Dick Hepinstall came into the club and sat next to him. "Hello, Mr Hepinstall. I'm surprised to see you in here. How are you?"

"You can drop the 'Mr' bit now, William. Dick it is from now on. I see you're from Aspull, which I knew well twenty odd years ago. I'm originally from Westhoughton."

"Well, Dick, thanks. That's two surprises in the one day, although I do recognise your accent as not being too far from Aspull. We don't see much of you these days. I suppose there are still even more newcomers arriving every week?"

"There are indeed William. They're coming from all over Europe, mainly from Poland right now. But I'm not just here for the beer. I've come with some news for you about a new house that's just been completed. It's a bungalow like the others, but this one has three bedrooms, so it's ideal for your family when they arrive. The address is 38 Argyll Street."

"Well, thank goodness for that. I was beginning to worry we might not have somewhere to live, and I'm sure they'll be here early in the new year. We've never had a house that size before. Thank you."

"Yes, I know. You'll be anxious to see the place, I'm sure. So what if I meet you here tomorrow, same time? I'll have the keys and take you up there."

William stood and shook hands with Dick. "That's very kind of you, Dick. It's a great relief I can tell you."

The house in Argyll Street came already furnished with beds, table, and chairs, even down to bedding and towels. Anything else was down to William to provide.

He worked all through Christmas, which was welcomed by all the men with families. And the extra money helped with shopping for things in the house before Elizabeth's arrival. It would mainly be a question of making sure there was enough food and that the house was warm enough when they arrived in two weeks' time.

William took time out on Sunday and met Jimmy and Peter in the club to compare notes on their preparations to welcome their wives. "Other than things like milk, bread, and fresh vegetables, I think I've bought in enough to last a month, although I'm sure to have missed lots. What about you, Jimmy?"

"Same here, William. Not sure about Peter here. You seem to be pretty relaxed about it all."

Peter was quiet, deep in thought, for a change. "I'm getting quite excited at seeing them all again after this time. But I can't help wondering how they will react to a new country, a new home, and a totally different way of life. After all, it's too late now to change their minds."

William was surprised hearing such a profound statement coming from Peter. He never seemed to have a care in the world. He was the joker in the pack.

"We're all in the same boat, Pete," Jimmy replied.

The overnight train was due at ten o'clock, and William had been waiting at the station in Union Street well before nine. When it did eventually arrive, it was only half an hour late. Elizabeth had travelled all the way from Lancashire with Ellen, aged three and a half, and little John, not quite eighteen months. William was sure that life must have been very hard for her during the past twelve months and then having to face leaving family and friends to sail all the way to Canada. Hard seemed something of an understatement.

It was several minutes before he spotted Elizabeth carrying a suitcase and, of course, her handbag. He didn't immediately connect that there was no sign of the children but ran forward to meet her. In a moment, their arms were wrapped around each other, and they kissed repeatedly.

Tears of happiness rolled down Elizabeth's cheeks. "Oh, my love, here at last. I can hardly believe I'm here." She gasped. "I missed you so much William. How are you?"

"I'm doing fine my love, but what about you? Where are the children?"

"Luckily, I've had the company of two friends all the way from Wigan. I would have found it impossible to manage without their help."

Elizabeth turned to her two companions and introduced them in turn. "William, you already know Jimmy's wife, Dorothy, and you told me you're already in touch with him."

Dorothy smiled and held out little John so that William could give him a big hug. Baby John cried so was promptly handed back to Dorothy. "Thanks, Dorothy." He'd almost forgotten about crying babies.

Elizabeth then turned to her other companion, who was holding baby Ellen. "And this is Jennie Spellman, Peter's wife."

"Thank you. Thank you both," was all he could say.

William hugged Ellen tightly, and although she didn't cry, she frowned, not sure who this strange man was. "There's lots off work with flu at the moment, so that both Jimmy and Peter have had to work the afternoon shift. That's why it's only me here. So, if you come home with us, they'll come for you straight from the pit as soon as they finish."

Later, both families, including the two Gregory babies, had a meal together at 38 Argyll Street before the Makinsons and Spellmans went off to their new homes.

The period following the happy reunion was, in William's experience, the longest uninterrupted and happiest period he could remember since they were married. Baby Henry was born in 1908, and Angus, two years later in 1910. Now with a family of six,

William and Elizabeth found life in Canada had turned out to be much better than either could ever have imagined.

Their happiness seemed to be complete when, in September 1911, Elizabeth gave birth to another baby girl, who they named Christy Ann. However completely happy they were with the growing family, like all good things in life, this was not destined to last forever. At only six months of age, baby Christy Ann died in her sleep, and from no apparent cause.

CHAPTER 6

Clouds on the Horizon

1914

EVERY JUNE FOR the past six years, the children of school age were allowed two free weeks while their teachers took some time out. This had usually given William and Elizabeth the chance to take the children out exploring the region during daytimes, returning home early evening.

However, this year, William had been switched to the early shift for a month while a number of workers were in hospital as a result of an accident at the pit. Elizabeth had still been able to take the children out with the support of Dorothy and Jennie, as always.

At the end of William's shift, he met Jimmy Makinson in the pit yard. "How are you doing,

Jimmy? I see that Dorothy is helping Elizabeth out again today."

"Yes, she is. All three wives seem to get on so well together. I think they're a good help to each other," he replied. "I'm glad we're here, though the folks back home must be worried about the situation in Europe. I remember only too well how your dad always followed the news."

"Why's that, Jimmy? Am I missing something then?"

"You surely are. Haven't you seen yesterday's paper then, William?"

"No. What's happened, Jimmy?"

"It's really worrying, William. I'm surprised Elizabeth hasn't heard. Well, according to the paper, on 28 June, Archduke Franz Ferdinand of Austria was assassinated in Sarajevo. Sounds like real trouble at t' mill if you ask me."

"Sarajevo, Jimmy?"

"The paper says it's in Bosnia. Anyway, I guess we haven't heard the last of this affair. Are you having a swift one in the club before you go home then?"

"Not today, Jimmy. I'll be off straight away. Maybe on Friday perhaps—payday, you know."

At War with Germany

Just over a month later, as William was leaving for work on the early shift, he saw his next-door neighbour, Ken Hall, just closing his front door. "Morning, William," Ken said. "You heard the news?"

"No. What's that then, Ken?"

"We're at war with Germany. Apparently, Prime Minister Asquith confirmed the declaration in London yesterday afternoon."

"So I wonder where that leaves us now?" William asked.

"I'm sure it means that we're in it as well. God help us all I say."

"Just what I didn't want to hear right now, Ken. Obviously, Elizabeth doesn't know yet, but I'm sure she will by the time we get back home this afternoon. Come on then. We'd better be off now."

In the next two years, life became increasingly difficult for everyone. Not only was there pressure to increase coal output for industrial and domestic consumption at home, but also, with the formation of the Canadian Expeditionary Force, the demand for greater numbers of men resulted in fewer being available to work in industry, and coal mining in particular.

Dick Hepinstall called a meeting in the club early one evening. At least a dozen others were there along with William, Jimmy, and Peter. "It's to state the obvious that the war is affecting us all and our families more as time passes," Dick said. "The urgent need for more recruits into the armed forces is resulting in manpower shortages throughout industry and, locally, the pit. Desperate times call for desperate measures, as the saying goes. I'm sure it won't be long before women and children will have to work, the same as it is back home."

Jimmy raised his hand to attract Dick's attention. "We're all putting in extra hours as it is. So, if it becomes necessary, how soon do you think the wives and kids will have to work at the pit?"

"All I can say right now, Jimmy, is that management is already talking about it. So fairly soon is the answer."

As had always been the case back in Lancashire, women and children in Cape Breton were now to be seen doing jobs previously undertaken by men. In turn, both Ellen and then John would have to leave school and go to work at the pit.

At least once every month, there could be heard the sound of a military band marching through the streets of Sydney ahead of a group of veterans who were encouraging young men to volunteer for service in Europe. The Lord Kitchener poster, "Your Country Needs You", so familiar to everyone back in the United Kingdom, had now been adopted throughout Canada and was to be seen on every public building and even at the pit gates.

Just after Christmas 1915, William was settled for the evening—much like his dad had done back home—enjoying his pipe and reading the *Cape Breton Post*. "Not much local news this week. It's all about the war."

"I met Dorothy Makinson and Jennie Spellman in the shop today," said Elizabeth.

"Did you? How were they?" William turned his attention back to the paper, deep in thought.

Elizabeth continued. "Have you seen Jimmy or Pete lately, William?"

"Not since just before Christmas, love. In fact, not since we went to that meeting with Dick Hepinstall. Why's that?"

"Well. Dorothy told me that they've both joined the army and will be leaving by the end of February."

"Never! I know we've been on different shifts, but I'm surprised they didn't come round to tell me." William dropped the paper, relit his pipe, stood, and walked around the room, shaking his head. He was shocked to hear this news.

"I would have thought that was the least they should have done. Jennie told me they're joining the Cape Breton Highlanders."

"Yes. The paper says that a lot of men from Sydney are going to the regiment, only a few to the navy. There'll soon be no young men left. Good luck to them, I'm sure."

William had known Jimmy since they were at school together. His dad, Frank, had worked with William's at one time. And although he hadn't really gotten to know Peter well until they met in the pit clubhouse here in Sydney, he had known his uncle Harold Spellman during the time he worked on the trams in Wigan.

In the coming weeks, William took the children down to the station to see the Highlander's Pipes and Drums leading the recruiting teams. The boys found it all very exciting, although Ellen stayed indoors with her mam. "Makes you feel proud to see them, don't you think?"

"Yes Dad," the boys replied in unison.

On Sunday evening after dinner, William and Elizabeth sat at the kitchen table with a cup of tea before bed. "You've been very quiet today love. Is there anything troubling you?" Elizabeth asked.

William took a deep breath in to release something that had been playing on his mind for weeks. "We were talking about the war at work earlier today. They're bringing a lot of the olduns out of retirement to work at the pit."

"Yes, I know. Times are hard right now. Even our two will be working before we know it."

William hesitated and then blurted it out. "How would you feel if I enlisted like the others?"

This came as no real surprise to Elizabeth. She had thought for some time that this was inevitable, sooner or later. "Well, if you feel you have to go, of course you'll have my support, love. But don't you think you might be too old?"

"No. I don't think so. Some as old as forty are going. I hate the thought of leaving you and the children behind yet again. But sad to say, I think I have little choice in the matter. I have come to think of the war as fighting for the future freedom of the whole world, and I don't want our children to grow up in a Canada ruled by Germans. I have to go."

The following day, on his way home after finishing the early shift, William called into the Sydney recruiting office to volunteer. The recruiting sergeant by the name of Scanlon, seemed very pleased to see him. "Good to see a more mature man stepping forward to do his duty, Mr Gregory. If you wouldn't mind completing your details on this registration form. You will then receive a letter in the near future giving details of when to report back here. Generally, it takes about two weeks. Then you'll be given a medical examination, and when you've signed the attestation, you will have become a member of the finest regiment in the Canadian Army and, needless to say, the finest army in the world."

The letter arrived two days later.

CHAPTER 7

You're in the Army Now

WILLIAM'S LAST SHIFT at the pit was the Saturday morning, 11 March 1916, a week before his thirty-seventh birthday. On the following Monday, Carl Sparrow from the *Cape Breton Post* called and took a photograph of all the family outside the house. Both William and Elizabeth were to keep a copy of the picture close to their hearts while ever they were apart.

William Elizabeth and children outside
their home at 38 Argyll Street.

On Wednesday morning, William went to the recruiting office at ten o'clock as required in the letter. The sergeant rifled through the pile of papers on his desk and then picked out William's form. "Right now. Follow me." In the back room, he was given a physical examination by the medical officer, who declared him fit for service.

Back in the main office, William signed the attestation form and swore the oath of allegiance to the king, and then the sergeant stood and shook his hand. "Congratulations, Private Gregory. You are now posted to the 185th Battalion Nova Scotia Rifles, Cape Breton Highlanders. You're in the army now."

William wasn't yet to know that would be the last time anyone in the army above the rank of private would be quite so friendly.

"You're now free to go home. But you must report back here for duty at 0700 hours on Monday, 27 March. From here, you'll be taken by battalion transport to Broughton Camp, where you will be met by the NCO who will be in charge of your training.

"Take only the clothes you're wearing and your washing and shaving kit. Your clothes will be returned to your wife after you've been issued your uniform and other equipment. Here's your ID card. Guard it as though your very life depended on it, and at some point in time, it might well do that. I've no doubt you will be granted leave to come home from time to time before you get posted overseas, so it's not exactly saying goodbye to your family. Anyway, for the time being, good luck."

So, William had a whole ten days free to spend with Elizabeth and the children. It was rare that, as a family, they were able to spend so much time together, and William was determined to make the most of it.

On Sunday evening when all the children were in bed, there was time to talk about the arrangements for the family during William's absence. "The army will pay a weekly allowance into your post office account, just as the pit did when I first arrived in Glace Bay. Everything else will carry on as normal. The house, your health care, and the children's education are all taken care of by the government."

"That certainly was a worry, until Jimmy and Peter joined up. Then the girls told me all about it. Now promise me you'll write every day, William. We need to know you're safe and in good health."

"You know I'll do my best to write as often as I can love," he replied.

Fortunately, on Monday morning the children were still asleep as William said goodbye to Elizabeth at the front door. Halfway down the street, he turned and waved, and Elizabeth returned a brief half wave goodbye before she ran inside, trying not to show her tears in front of the children.

At the recruiting office, William was met by the sergeant and six other new recruits waiting for the transport. The truck picked them up half an hour later, and as William was the eldest, he got in the cab alongside the driver.

After the short journey to Broughton, they pulled into what used to be the pit yard. As they stopped, William pointed at the giant of a man in uniform watching as the truck slowed to a halt and parked on the edge of the yard. He was every inch the military figure William had imagined—well over six feet tall, handlebar moustache, ramrod straight back, and barrel-chested. "Who's that over there then?" he asked.

"That's Sar'nt MacKay. He'll be your training instructor. Better all get down now. He's not the most patient of men."

As William and the others dismounted, they were greeted by the loudest voice any of them had ever heard before. "Right, you lot. Gather up your belongings and form a straight line here. From now on, you are no longer a line or a row but a rank."

The giant with three stripes took a deep breath in, "*What are you?*" he bellowed.

"A rank, sir," they replied as one.

"Now, if you gentlemen wouldn't mind," the sergeant asked in a fairly quiet but sarcastic tone, "*Form three ranks of twelve*! Tallest on the right, shortest on the left."

After much shuffling and bumping into each other, the men eventually made three ranks.

"Move your bodies. Listen in. This used to be the pit yard, but it is now the training depot drill square." He paced up and down, stopping and looking each man from head to foot before continuing. "My name is Sergeant Talbot MacKay, and my mother calls me Talbot ... or son." He then took another deep breath in before bellowing even louder than before, "But you boys—*you will call me sergeant*! When I've finished with you, you pathetic excuses for men, I will have turned you into real Highland fighting men, honoured to belong to the finest infantry regiment on earth."

At that moment, every man in the ranks would surely have echoed William's inner feelings that Sergeant MacKay had put the fear of God in everyone. *But it's too late now*, he thought. *There's no turning back!*

"Now you're going to turn to your left. And for those of you who don't know left from right, your arse from your elbow, *this is left.*" He pointed his stick again to emphasise the point.

Another deep breath in, and Sar'nt MacKay's chest swelled, "*Leeefftt turn!*"

All three ranks turned to their left as best they could.

"By the right, *quick march!*"

Hard as they might try to follow, it was more like a shuffle than marching.

"Get a move on; I haven't got all day to waste."

They "marched" across the yard, trying their best to keep in step, heading towards the old buildings that had been converted into accommodation for the recruits. As they continued, it looked as though they were headed straight into the nearest building until Sarn't MacKay bellowed, "Squad. Squaard halt!"

This, the unhappy band of warriors took to be an order to stop marching. Some stopped in their tracks, while others continued, and the whole squad of thirty-six ended up falling over each other in a heap.

"*Stand up. Stand still!*" Sar'nt MacKay screamed. "Heaven help us. What have I done to deserve you lot? Anyway, Corporal Jackson's on his way over to take you on from here."

Much to their relief, Sarn't MacKay left them as they were trying to reassemble in some form of order.

Corporal Jackson proved to be every bit as fearsome as the drill sergeant. He spent the next quarter of an hour checking everyone's details for yet another time. Then he took them to the barbershop, where they all had an extra short haircut. Finally, they were off to the quartermaster's stores, where they were issued with a Highland beret; a Black Watch tartan kilt and matching long socks; and a khaki shirt, battledress jacket and trousers, leather boots, and puttees.

It was ten thirty by the time they all got back to the barrack room and the welcome sight of rows of iron bed frames covered with wooden boards down both sides. Corporal Jackson lit a couple of candles to give off some light but then disappeared without another word.

The bed frames were so inviting after such a long day that two or three of the men just dropped their kits and stretched their legs out on the bare boards. This proved to be the biggest mistake they could possibly have made, as the sound of boots on the stairs could be heard approaching two minutes before Sar'nt MacKay burst through the door. "Get off those beds right now, or I'll chop your lazy legs off and feed them to the pigs at the farm!" he yelled, although not quite as loudly as he had when he was on the square.

It had an immediate effect, and even after a few short hours they had already learned to stand to attention the moment the drill sar'nt appeared.

"It's been a long day, but there's more to do before you get some sleep. On each bed, there's a sack, and what you do is to put all your civilian clothes in it and write your number, rank, and name on the label. They will be sent to your next of kin tomorrow. The piper will sound reveille at 0630 hours in the morning, and I expect you all to be washed, shaved, and dressed by seven. Then after breakfast at 0730, be on the drill square at 0900 hours sharp, fully dressed in your new uniform and with all your equipment. From there, we will be marching to the station, and then by train to CFB Valcartier."

"Valcartier? Where's that, Sar'nt MacKay?" a voice from the other end of the room enquired.

"CFB. That's the Canadian Forces Base, Valcartier, north west of Quebec. It's where you'll undergo your basic training over the next three months. After that, you can truly say you are a Highlander and ready for action. "Now fill your mattress covers from the pile of straw over in the far corner, dowse the candles, and get yourselves to bed." With that, he was gone.

William was exhausted. He stuffed some straw into the mattress cover, took his boots off, rolled onto the bed, and pulled the blanket over his head.

As for his promise to write to Elizabeth every day, it wouldn't take long before he came to realise that letter writing would have to be whenever time allowed.

CHAPTER 8

Coming of Age

TWO DAYS LATER, William and the other new recruits arrived by road transport at the Valcartier training area. They dismounted on the parade ground, an open area surrounded on three sides by row upon row of bell tents.

As soon as they'd picked up their kit bags, they were called by a quartermaster sar'nt. "In single file, follow me, and I'll show you where to find your allocated accommodation in Charlie Four; that's the fourth row back from the parade ground."

Five minutes later, they arrived at a large wooden sign marked "C4—2Pl". This left little chance for getting lost.

"Ten to a tent. Dump your gear on the floor and then look sharp back to the square. Sarn't MacKay is there now to welcome you to CFB. You have five minutes."

"Some kind of welcome that is," Tam MacLeish muttered under his breath.

Back at the parade ground, sure enough, Sar'nt MacKay was waiting for them. "Right now, you are in Row 4 Charlie Company, and 2 Platoon will be in these four bell tents here. Remember that this is now the place where you will be sleeping in these first three, so be sensible and keep your gear nice and tidy. I'll be next door in the fourth with two other platoon sar'nts. You'll find the training here pretty tough, with the emphasis on physical fitness and weapons drills on the ranges at Hart Hill. A word of warning, though. Be careful with the Ross rifle, which has a few problems and has a habit of surprising you with stoppages. Let's hope we get the go-ahead to switch to the Lee Enfield soon. If you apply yourselves to the training, you'll find that the time here will seem to fly by."

And so it was that the following days quickly turned into weeks, and soon their time at Valcartier was up. To mark the end of the twelve-week training, there was a passing out parade, at which the CFB commandant took the salute. After marching off the square, they were ordered to report to the orderly room, where they were issued with rail warrants to return home for ten days' embarkation leave.

William had been at home for four of his ten days, and they had so far avoided talking about the future. In the evening after all the children were in bed, they would sit in the kitchen and talk about the letters from home in Aspull and how the children had been so well-behaved and such great support to Elizabeth whilst he was away. In fact, they would usually discuss anything except the future after his leave ended.

William reached for Elizabeth's hand across the table. "Tomorrow's halfway through my leave, and we haven't even thought about what happens next, Elizabeth."

"Well, I've thought about it. But I suppose I'd rather not dwell on what the future might hold when you're posted to France. Let's just make the most of the rest of your leave. You know the children have loved having you back home again for a while."

All too soon it was time for William to be back in uniform, and they were saying goodbye once again. This was something that by now they were well used to. Only for Elizabeth, this time it was with a strange sense of foreboding that she watched as he marched down the street towards the town hall where the transport was waiting to take them back to Broughton.

The following day, the platoon was formed up on the square as the adjutant approached them from the direction of the headquarters building, accompanied by the chief clerk. They stopped briefly at each man. William was in the middle of the centre rank, waiting his turn.

"Name?" the adjutant asked.

"It's 877776 Private Gregory, sir," William replied.

The adjutant turned to the colour sergeant, who checked his list. "Bravo Company 25th Battalion, sir."

"Right, Gregory. Fallout and join the others in front of the mess hall."

William turned to his right and then marched off to join the group on the edge of the square in front of the mess. There were a couple of faces he recognised from working at the pit in Glace Bay, and he assumed this must be the group joining Bravo Company. Others were peeling off and gathering in front of the accommodation block, so they must be going to another battalion.

Having now completed basic training, it was noticeable how easily they instinctively formed three ranks and stood at ease awaiting the next word of command. They didn't have to wait long before they were to be surprised yet again as the familiar figure of Sar'nt MacKay could be seen marching in their direction. Then the equally familiar command, "Platoon. Platoon, attention!"

And as though they were one, the three ranks sprang to attention.

"I bet you weren't expecting to see me again so soon. How lucky can you be?" There was no response.

William was certainly shocked to be confronted by Sar'nt MacKay once more. They had all assumed he was on the permanent training staff. Everyone else was surely thinking the same.

"This morning I was posted from the training camp staff to the 25th Battalion, and with immediate effect I am your platoon sergeant, and you are now 6 Platoon, Bravo Company.

"I know that the company commander and CSM Rose are looking forward to your arrival and bringing the company up to full strength. Alpha and Charley passed through here two weeks ago. We're going from here back to the CFB training area, where we expect to receive our orders before the end of August for sailing to the UK. After that, we go to France, wherever we're needed. That's when we're going to see some real action, my boys.

"I told you before we first went to CFB that you would make fine Highlanders, and so you have. You're now a platoon anyone would be proud to lead."

Overcoming the initial shock, they hesitated, as Sar'nt MacKay took a deep breath in and then snarled. "Are you ready for it?" Then, *"I said, are you ready for it?"*

"Yes, Sar'nt," they replied as one.

Pointing with his stick, as usual, he added, "You see those two trucks parked in front of the HQ block?"

"Yes, Sar'nt."

"Well, I give you two minutes to get on board. We leave in five."

Today was a special day for new surprises, and as William turned towards the waiting transport at least a hundred yards away, he instantly recognised Jimmy and Peter Spellman. He'd know those smiles anywhere. "Jimmy. Pete! How on earth did you get here? I thought you'd been posted to another battalion? It's good to see you both again."

There followed some vigorous handshaking and backslapping between the three reunited pals. Jimmy was the first to explain. "We enquired about you at the recruiting office, and as Sar'nt Scanlon is a mate of Sar'nt MacKay, he fixed it for us to join the 25th Battalion, same company, same platoon."

"That's great news Jimmy, so that we can be together again. When I asked after you two, Sar'nt Scanlon didn't seem to know much, except that the last he' heard was when you went to Broughton. Where did you go after that?"

"We went to CFB as you did, except that when we completed our training our group was attached to the Valcartier Demo Company for three months."

"So that's where you were. What exactly does a demonstration company do then, Pete?"

"Well, it's a good number of things really, William. On major exercises, we acted as enemy; gives you a good idea about the conditions in France. The only drawback as far as I'm concerned is that we didn't get any time off. I know Jimmy agrees with me on that score. Now we're back there again, we're pretty sick of the place. And still no time off."

From April through to the end of the third week of August, the whole battalion was under canvas at Valcartier. Base camp was established some fifteen miles north of the main training facility and three miles from the nearest road. William and the rest of the platoon were in bivouacs in a heavily wooded area some two miles from company headquarters.

It was during this period that William came to recognise a totally different side to Sar'nt MacKay, and with only a couple of exceptions, most of 6 Platoon came to respect his leadership qualities. William wrote in a letter to Elizabeth, "There are times when he reveals an almost human side of his nature."

At the end of August as they were assembled on the square waiting for transport to take them back to the station, Company Commander Major Heywood addressed them. "Well done, men. Due to the early deployment of other units, we've been here much longer than planned, but then, we are so much better prepared as a result. The time we have spent here at the training facility has sadly been marred by a number of accidents, including two deaths in Alpha Company. I now feel that we are ready for the planned deployment to France in the next two to three months. I am also able to tell you that, when we arrive back in Halifax, you will have a further five days leave to return to your homes to say your goodbyes. Today is also probably the last you'll see of me, as I've been posted to 2 Division HQ in France. So goodbye and good luck. Captain McInnis will now fill you in with more detail about your future movements. Cheerio, all." The major saluted and then went to the transport waiting for him.

The second in command saluted in reply before Major Heywood's driver whisked him off and out of sight.

Captain McInnis moved to the front of the platoon. "Right. Now listen up. The latest news I have is that we are due to set sail from Halifax bound for Liverpool on 12 October, when the whole brigade will march through the streets of Sydney before boarding the ship RMS *Olympic* in Halifax. From Liverpool, the company will move by train to Witley Camp, which is near Godalming in Surrey. There, you will undertake final preparations for posting overseas. Carry on, Sar'nt Major."

Salutes exchanged, Captain McInnis marched off.

Back home at the end of the final spell of leave, the children were woken at 6 a.m. on the Monday morning to say goodbye to their father. Elizabeth cried; the children cried; and as much as he tried, William was also on the verge of tears.

None of them knew when they might next meet. Elizabeth lined the children up to say goodbye to their Dad, and he gave each one a kiss and a big hug. He stopped and patted John on the cheek, "Now son you're the man of the house while I'm away. So make sure to look after your mam, little Angus, and your sisters."

"I will Dad. I promise." John looked up at William, trying his very best to withhold the tears welling up inside him. This was indeed a considerable responsibility for a boy of ten.

On the doorstep, as she waved goodbye, Elizabeth's parting words were, "Remember, my love, you promised to write whenever you can. And I will do the same."

CHAPTER 9

About-Turn

THE RMS *OLYMPIC* sailed from Halifax for the United Kingdom on 12 October 1916. Throughout the trip, the battalion's schedule consisted largely of an hour's PT each morning and afternoon, rifle drills, kit inspections, and lectures about life in the trenches from officers who had been at either Ypres or Loos in 1915.

With some time on their hands in the evening, many in the platoon took the opportunity to ask Sar'nt MacKay about his experiences in the Second Battle of Ypres in April 1915. He didn't encourage it, though, as most still believed they were embarked on some great adventure. He felt it much better they should continue to feel that way, as the harsh reality of life at the front would seem only too real soon enough.

Trenchard, in Number 2 Rifle Section, normally

a man of few words, surprised William one night while they were in the mess. "For me, I think it was the second spell at Valcartier that I began to see another side to Sar'nt MacKay. In my opinion, he's come up trumps in the end, and he's certainly gained everyone's respect for what he's done for us."

"I totally agree with you," replied William. "What do you say, Pete?"

Peter smiled and nodded in agreement.

A week later, the *Olympic* docked in Liverpool. And while back in Canada, many things seemed to be constantly changing, William wasn't at all surprised to see that virtually nothing had changed here since he'd left a little over ten years earlier.

Once all had assembled on the dockside, the quartermaster came to speak to everyone. "The latest news is that the accommodation at Witley Camp will not now be available for at least two weeks. So in the meantime, the battalion will be moving by train and road transport to a temporary tented camp at Pirbright, which is also in Surrey, not far from Witley."

Two days later at Pirbright, Sar'nt MacKay gathered 6 Platoon together to pass on the arrangements regarding meals, washing facilities, and security. "The camp staff has placed great emphasis on the need for maintaining extra security due to the recent threat from Irish Republicans."

Even bearing in mind the heightened security threat, it didn't come as a great surprise when on their second night Peter Spellman found his way out of the restricted area and headed for The White Hart pub in Pirbright village where he got very drunk and became involved in a fight with some locals. The MPs were called to sort out the brawl, and they locked him up for the night in the regimental police hut.

At commanding officer's orders the following morning, Pete was awarded ten days CB (confined to barracks) which everyone thought was hilarious as all movement was in any case already meant to be confined to within the perimeter of the camp.

Later that day, William was talking to Jimmy Makinson and Jack Hodson about the affair. "Sod's Law has it that I wouldn't be at all surprised that, when his ten days are up, he'd have at least one more go at escaping to the pub again. But in any case, I think he's safe as we'll probably be in Witley before he gets the chance. Don't know what the problem is. He never used to be that fond of drink."

"Otherwise, I would have put money on that

happening. What I mean is Pete getting drunk, not the move to Witley," said Jimmy.

Witley Camp

It was late on Wednesday afternoon three weeks later when the company eventually left Pirbright for Witley Camp and 2200 hours before they found their accommodation. Peter Spellman hadn't stopped complaining all day about almost everything. "What a welcome this is—dark, cold, raining, no food or hot drinks."

"What's wrong then Pete? It's just not like you to be so miserable."

William felt much the same. There wasn't a great deal to be cheerful about, but moaning wasn't going to change anything.

Jimmy put his arm round Pete's shoulder. "We'll soon be indoors and drying out, and I'm sure there'll at least be a hot brew going soon. In any case, you won't see the platoon sar'nt unhappy about things. In fact, I'm sure he'd say that cold, wet, and hungry is exactly how it's going to be when we get to France."

"I suppose so," Peter grudgingly admitted.

Inside the hut, there were fifteen beds down each side, with a separate bunk at the end reserved for the platoon sar'nt. Washing and latrines were in the hut next door.

Sar'nt MacKay returned from a briefing in the camp headquarters. "Find yourselves a bed space. Leave your gear on the bed. And follow Corporal Jackson here to the cookhouse, where you can at least get a mug of fresh tea. I expect lamps out and everyone in bed by 2330 hours at the latest. You've got all day tomorrow to get yourselves sorted."

The Platoon Sar'nt was as tired out as everyone and was unusually quiet.

Hopefully, the following day would prove to be free as promised and there would be plenty of time to get organised and familiar with the camp, time for William to write to Elizabeth and Mam in Aspull.

They all felt better having had a mug of hot tea, and Peter Spellman was now his old cheerful, jokey self. William put his kit bag at the end of the bed, hung his uniform from the overhead shelf, and quickly fell into a deep sleep.

As promised, Sunday was pretty relaxed, with reveille at 0700 hours and breakfast an hour later. The Padre held a short service at ten o'clock, after which they were free for the rest of the day.

After church parade, Sar'nt MacKay called them together in the barrack room. "Make the most of today and remember this is a training establishment. So you're not allowed off camp. And no strolling around casually with your hands in your pockets. I expect you to march smartly, although at your own pace. Be back in your beds by 2200 hours and at your best come Monday morning. Understood?"

"Yes, Sar'nt," most replied.

The platoon sar'nt came over to William. "Now, Gregory. You are to report to battalion HQ at 1030 hours tomorrow to attend commanding officer's orders."

"What's that for, Sar'nt?" William asked.

"I'm not at liberty to say what it's for. You just make sure you're there on time." Unusually, Sar'nt MacKay was smiling as he turned and went back to his bunk.

The following morning, the piper sounded reveille at 0600 hours. Having washed, shaved, and dressed in PT order, Sar'nt MacKay led the platoon out on their first run at Witley. This at least gave them a glimpse of the world outside of the camp.

"A short run to get some fresh air in those lungs and then back for breakfast at 0700. After that, the platoon commander will address you about your training here at Witley before we start."

Compared with Valcartier, the run was relatively

short, probably only about three miles, but it certainly got the legs moving again after a few weeks of relative inactivity. Then, breakfast over, they cleaned up the barrack room before the platoon commander arrived, and spot on 0815 the door opened and Lieutenant Bell came into the room, smiling as usual.

Sar'nt MacKay saluted and at the same time ordered, "Number 6 Platoon present as ordered, sir."

"Thank you Sar'nt MacKay. Stand the men at ease."

The platoon commander paced up and down the room, carefully inspecting each man and each bed space, "Right, now, welcome to Witley Camp, where we will train in readiness for the call forward to France. When, of course, we don't yet know. However, we will make the most of our time here, training in conditions as close to those at the front as is possible. While you're here, I remind you all that you are being watched by other units, as well as the Witley permanent staff. So, be on your best behaviour at all times and present yourselves and the regiment in the best possible light to everyone you meet. That's all for now. Carry on, Sar'nt MacKay."

At 1020 hours, William reported to the drill sergeant at battalion headquarters. "Sir, 877776 Private Gregory."

The drill sergeant's eagle eye looked him up and down. "Stand over there until you're called Gregory."

Ten minutes later he was marched in by the RSM and halted in front of the commanding officer.

"Private Gregory, B Company 6 Platoon, sir."

The CO looked at a report on his desk. "I'm pleased to say that we've watched your progress over recent months Gregory. And in particular as the men of 6 Platoon are all so much younger than yourself, it has been noted that they show you a great degree of respect. As a result, your Platoon Commander has recommended your promotion to lance corporal, and I have today endorsed that recommendation. Congratulations. Well done. March out, Sar'nt Major."

An hour later, William rejoined the platoon as the men were on their way back to the huts from drill on the square. Everyone gathered round to admire the lance corporal's chevron newly sewn onto William's sleeve.

Jimmy and Peter were the first to shake his hand. "Long overdue in my opinion. Don't you think so Jimmy?"

"'I certainly do Pete. Now, we have some news for you while you were down at HQ, William."

"What've I missed then? Other than an hour on the square I mean."

"It was more like half an hour's drill today, William. The platoon commander came with the news that the Ross rifle has finally been withdrawn from service, and we're getting the .303 Lee Enfield. We're restricted to the camp for the next four weeks, although we can walk out after that on Sundays for church."

The training schedule at Witley was much the same as at Pirbright, but there was no denying that they were now very fit and enjoying live firing on the range with the Lee Enfield.

However monotonous the routine was during the first three months, there were two incidents William would never forget. They were, therefore, well worth recording in his journal:

22 November 1916

> Corporal of the guard for the first time last night. Sergeant McDonald sent me with Private Murphy to break up a fight on the road outside the accommodation lines—Peter Spellman again. Wilson ended up in the hospital. Not too serious,

though, and I'd always thought they were best of pals. Wilson had started the argument so only had himself to blame. Pete had not been drinking!

I had been told that the guard duty at Witley only came round every six months so expected only to have to do one while we're here. So much then for a guard every six months. It's now less than a month since my first guard and just finished my second, patrolling the camp perimeter with the staff regimental police sergeant, Sar'nt Woodburn. He's a tall, thin man and immaculately turned out at all times. He didn't say much but simply pointed with his pace stick. Everything seemed quiet until we came to the MT yard and the long line of parked trucks, when he spotted a light shining through the tarpaulin at the back of one of the vehicles. He pulled the cover back and went crazy at the sight of someone holding a lamp, and all I could see was a bare backside. His shout must have been heard miles away, and the horses tethered next to the wagons were startled and made a helluva racket.

Two privates from the Royal Hampshires jumped down, and Sar'nt Woodburn immediately ordered me to lock them up in the guardroom. Just as I was about to march the prisoners off, the terrified face of a woman appeared at the back of the vehicle.

Sar'nt Woodburn poked the woman with his stick and told her to stay where she was. I marched the prisoners off to the guardroom so never found out what happened to the woman. I could hazard a pretty good guess though.

His diary entry 12 December 1916 recorded Bravo Company's turn to attend a briefing by the Battalion 2IC Major MacLeod in the main mess hall. MacLeod had been in action with the battalion earlier in the year at the St Eloi Craters and Sanctuary Wood. He wrote:

Apparently everywhere you go in France is a scene of absolute devastation with hardly a building or tree left intact. We will have to set our minds to seeing death and destruction everywhere. I suppose it's as well to be forewarned about what to expect. In the front line, there is a complicated network of trenches on both sides, much like those we train in almost every day here at Witley. Major MacLeod's final comments were to warn us never to allow ourselves to be taken prisoner, as the evil Hun do unspeakable things to POWs.

Back at the hut everyone sat either at the table or perched on bed ends talking about the lecture from the 2IC. Sar'nt MacKay pulled up a chair, anxious to hear the opinions about what had just been said. He told us that he had been at the Second Battle of Ypres, where he copped shrapnel in the left leg, was casevac to UK, and eventually ended up with the Halifax Armoury training staff.

William asked whether he knew what these unspeakable things are that the Hun do to their prisoners.

"Well, Corporal Gregory, let's put it this way. I

think it's best you don't know. Personally, I'd never allow myself to be taken alive. By the way, we always refer to Germans as Fritz. Any other questions?"

"That was all good stuff earlier I suppose, but what are the conditions really like Sergeant?" This time it was Jack Roberts asking the question and he very rarely said anything.

"Good question Roberts. I wondered when someone was going to ask that. Well, you should expect it to be cold and raining most of the time. Knee deep in mud, and you'll be pretty lousy with lice. Best to burn them off with a candle or a cigarette. The rats are a constant problem, and there doesn't seem to be much you can do about them other than put down the poison or traps. But they breed quicker than you can kill them. You will get the chance to clean up every few weeks when you have a break in billets to the rear. Well, that's all for now. Lamps out and all in bed in fifteen minutes."

If nothing else, this evening had given William and the rest of the platoon plenty to think about as they prepared for bed, their minds full of the move to Southampton tomorrow morning and what lay ahead when they arrived in France.

Over the following weeks, there was a new sense of expectation, as posting to France seemed imminent.

The weather had also turned very wintry—bitterly cold early mornings and late afternoons.

The battalion was then away from Witley for a week taking part in a brigade exercise on Salisbury Plain. And the day after they returned to Witley, everyone was issued with rail travel warrants for their Christmas leave. William wrote a long overdue letter to Elizabeth:

> 877776 L/Cpl Gregory W
> Witley Camp, Surrey
> 9 December 1916
> Dear Elizabeth,
>
> I can't say too much about what we've been doing, except to say that we have spent a great deal of time away training. You will probably all be surprised to see above that I have now been promoted to lance corporal, although I was happy enough as things were. The good news is that we have now been told that we have been given ten days leave from 18 December, which means I will be spending Christmas with the family in Aspull. Although I am very much looking

forward to seeing everyone, including your mam, I will miss not being with you and the children. I think of you every day. The next news is likely to be to tell you that we have been posted overseas at some time in the first few months of 1917. We have another very early start tomorrow, so it's off to bed shortly.

Thinking of you all the time.
With all my love,
William x

PS. We will be spending lots of time ankle deep in muddy water, which causes what they call trench foot, so it is important that we change socks every day. Please remember when you get the chance, I'm in need of socks!

Christmas in Aspull

It wasn't until the early hours of Monday 19 December that they arrived in Wigan. The journey from Godalming had taken eighteen hours in total, but it was worth being back in familiar surroundings. Of course, it was cold and raining steadily. *Nothing much changes around these parts*, thought William. Despite the rain, they were all headed in the same direction, so they set off walking together. William and Jimmy Makinson were headed for Aspull, while Peter Spellman and Ted Baker had farther to go, as far as Blackrod. When they got to the Aspull Finger Post, they separated and went their different ways.

William stopped at the corner of Stanley Road to check the time. Sure enough, it was half past five, and coming down the road was the usual crowd off to work, including Dad. He put his bag down and waited but said nothing. As the workers drew nearer, they seemed oblivious of the man in uniform stood at the corner watching.

As they were about to pass him, Jack Carter stopped and pointed. "Hey, John. I could swear that soldier over there looks like your William?"

"It is. It is. Well spotted, Jack."

John couldn't have been more surprised. "What on earth are you doing here son? We thought you were in Surrey."

William crossed the road and shook hands with his dad, and then they hugged. "Didn't you get my letter Dad? I'm home on leave for Christmas."

"Well. You'd better hurry up to see your mam. She certainly hasn't received any letter saying you were coming. Anyway, I have to go, otherwise I'll be late. But see you later on today son. It's so good to see you after all this time and looking so smart in your uniform." John turned and hurried to catch up with the others.

William had a full twelve days at home over Christmas and was determined to make the most of every moment. As he made his way up Stanley Road, he wondered why on earth his letter hadn't arrived in time to forewarn Mam of his imminent arrival.

However much he was looking forward to spending time with the family, he couldn't help feeling a sense of guilt that Elizabeth and the children would be spending their Christmas alone by themselves back in Sydney.

It only took a couple of minutes up Stanley Road, and instead of knocking on the front door, William went through the backyard; there wasn't a sound from either the hens or the pigeons, so he quietly opened the kitchen door to surprise Mam. She had her back to the door putting coal on the fire.

"Hello, Mam. I'm home."

Ellen turned and put her hand to her mouth, shocked to see William standing in the doorway. "What! Is that really you, William? Goodness, let me have a look at you now. So smart you are. And now a corporal, goodness me. I didn't know you were coming. I can't believe it. Your dad will be so pleased when he gets home from work." Ellen hugged him tightly. Tears of joy ran down her face.

"I've already seen Dad at the bottom of the street, Mam. I did write to tell you I was coming, but Dad said the letter hadn't arrived yet."

Ellen was already pouring water into the kettle. "Never mind. Let me make some tea and sit at the table. I want to know all your news. You'll be able to see Mrs Cubbin while you're here."

"Oh, I've lots to tell you, Mam. But what's been happening here?"

"Nothing much changes here, as you'll soon see. Bea has been very poorly with pneumonia for the past two weeks, but we didn't say anything as you've enough on your plate as it is."

"That is bad news, Mam. Do you think I'll be able to see her while I'm here?"

"I'm not at all sure that's a good idea, William. There's a lot of flu around at the moment, and the last thing we want is for you to go down with it. Of course, all her children have their own families now and have been taking good care of her."

Over the next couple of hours and with the teapot refreshed at least three times, William described as best he could everything that had happened in the past ten years since he and Elizabeth left. What a vast and beautiful country Canada was and generally how much their lives had been improved since they moved there. Ellen, of course, wanted to know all about the children, including Henry and Angus, who she had never seen.

By that evening, word of his arrival had spread quickly round the family, friends, and neighbours. The days that followed were filled with a constant stream of visitors. Of course, there was also plenty of time to catch up with Mam, Dad, and his sisters, but seldom on their own, as there never seemed to be any quiet time.

Leah came on Christmas Eve morning and spent an hour with William in the front room while Bertha entertained the children out back. Life had been extremely hard for her since Harry died. But in the years since then, everyone had, not surprisingly, been very kind to her and the children. As a result, she was now doing as well as could be expected in the circumstances. "We have a roof over our heads and food in the pantry, and although there isn't a day passes when I miss Harry so badly, it's not as painful as in the early days. Your mam has been wonderful and has kept us going through some pretty hard times."

"And that's as it should be, Leah. I mean that everyone should have pitched in and helped. I only wish we could have done more." William still missed Harry greatly.

Christmas Day was nice but quiet. The whole family ate together, and Leah came with the children. After dinner William went to see Mrs Cubbin. After he returned home, he wrote to Elizabeth with all the news:

26 Stanley Road, Aspull

25 December

Merry Christmas, my dearest Elizabeth. I've just returned from visiting your mam, who thankfully was in good health and spirit. She had dinner next door with the Ramsgate family, who, as you know, has always made sure she's not alone at Christmas ever since they moved from Clitheroe five years ago.

The whole family here sat down to dinner together, including Leah and the children, which was very nice. They all send you their love.

You'll remember mam's best friend, Bea Hardacre? She helped deliver me when I was born. Poor Bea is apparently very ill with pneumonia. I hope she gets better soon, please God. I wrote just before we left Witley Camp, so I'm sorry that you may not even have received the letter in time to know that I had been given leave. I wouldn't be surprised if you get both at the same time. But suffice to say that I have been thinking about you and how hard it must be managing on your own. I hope your friends have helped. God bless you all.

With all my love,
William x

All too soon, the Christmas festivities were over, and on Saturday, 30 December, William was once more back on the platform of Wigan Station. But there was no sign of the others. He assumed that perhaps they had already left or were taking the five o'clock train, in which case they wouldn't make it back to Witley until sometime tomorrow. Mam, Dad, and the girls went to see him off. The chat, as usual on these occasions, consisted of comments about the weather and how long everyone thought the journey might take.

They didn't have long to wait. It was no more than half an hour when the train pulled in. And after a quick hug and kiss all round and a firm handshake with Dad, William got on board and closed the door. He leant out of the window to wave goodbye. Mam and the girls cried. Dad was just quiet. They all waved until William lost sight of them.

It was midday on New Year's Eve when the train pulled into Euston Station, and it was early evening by the time William finally dropped his bag and bedding back in the 2 Platoon hut at Witley Camp.

There were quite a few men already back, especially those from Scotland. Most just lay quietly on their beds, remembering everything they had left behind and thinking about what lay ahead. There was no sign of the others from Wigan, so they had obviously caught the later train.

Suddenly, the barrack room door opened, and with a loud thud Sar'nt MacKay dropped his kit bag on the floor. "Welcome home, boys. I'm sure you all got used to the soft life again in the past couple of weeks." The oh-so-familiar swelling of the chest was followed by a louder than usual order, albeit this time with half a smile on his face. "Now get off your backsides and get on the back of the truck outside. You're going on a little trip."

William jumped up and walked towards the door, tapping each bed frame as he passed. Each man, in turn, got up somewhat reluctantly and followed him.

Half an hour later, the driver stopped outside a pub called the William IV. The men of 6 Platoon looked out, curious as to where they were and why were they here without waiting for the rest to return.

Sar'nt MacKay came round to the back of the vehicle with the driver. "Come on then. Look lively. Follow me."

With William leading, the men formed up in line and, after a fashion, marched to the pub entrance. The inside of the pub was full of locals, who were surprised to see the Canadian military invasion on their home territory. However, the landlord smiled and shook hands with Sar'nt MacKay. "Good to see you and the boys in Horsley Sergeant." He counted heads and then started pulling the beer pump. "Nine pints coming up then. Have this one on the house."

Over the next three hours they had six each, which for William was double the amount he would normally drink, and it hadn't cost them a penny. No one would ever know who paid. The regulars of West Horsley had certainly made them very welcome.

Back in camp by a quarter to eleven, they found that the rest of the platoon had arrived back while they had been enjoying themselves in the pub. The late returners were shattered after their journeys. The drinkers were unsteady and tired from too much ale. And Peter Spellman was beside himself with disappointment that the evening had ended when it did. It was not surprising that they were all under their blankets before midnight.

The Piper sounded reveille right outside 6 Platoon's hut at 0600 hours. William woke with a start and sat on the side of the bed, and on looking around the room, he couldn't see any movement from the others. Just as he was standing to wake everyone, the bunk door behind him opened. There was Sar'nt MacKay already washed, shaved, and dressed for the day, "Wakey. Wakey!" he bellowed.

Suddenly, there was movement all around the room, except for Pete Spellman—but not for long. The platoon sar'nt strode over and, in one swift move, upended the bed. Pete was now lying in a crumpled heap on the floor but definitely awake.

After breakfast, they went for a short run,

followed by stretching exercises and push-ups in the road outside the QM's store. Then they joined the end of a long queue into the store. No one seemed to know what they were waiting for. But all was soon revealed when they got inside, as the store man placed a gas mask in front of each man.

The rest of the day was spent in the practice trenches trying out the gas masks and getting familiar with the gas drill. Lt Bell joined them late morning while the platoon was taking a break to eat their haversack rations. "This afternoon we are all going to have our first experience of gas as used by the enemy. Don't be in any doubt that, unless your gas drill is perfect, you will be in serious trouble. If you don't react quickly and fit your mask properly, this poisonous gas will certainly cause severe vomiting and skin blisters, as well as badly damaging your eyes and lungs. In the worst case, it can even be fatal. Any questions?"

There were no questions. As to a man, they were all mulling over the effects of a gas attack. For the first time, it had dawned on them where all these months of training had been leading and that soon they would be fighting for their very lives, against gas as well as bullets and shellfire.

Sar'nt MacKay interrupted the silence. "I should

add that these gas trials involve the release of real chlorine gas but not enough to do you any harm unless you fail to put the training into practice."

The rest of the day's training passed without any problems, other than when Private Clarke threw up in the trench. However, this wasn't anything to do with gas but was certainly more to do with last night's trip to West Horsley.

Later, the platoon marched back to camp from the training area, arriving just in time for the 1700 meal in the cookhouse. Back in the room, William found a letter from Elizabeth on his bed. It was postmarked Christmas Eve. So the mail service had been better than expected for the time of year, and his first letter had obviously arrived in Glace Bay. It read:

> 38 Argyll Street
> Glace Bay, NS
> 23 December 1916
>
> Dearest William,
>
> Thank you for your letter. We were all pleased to hear of the news now you are a lance corporal and that you might spend Christmas with the family in Aspull.

I hope this finds you in good health. And with only a few more days to go until it's Christmas, the children and I wonder what you will be doing during the festive season. We all miss you so much, and this first Christmas without you will be very lonely. I know it would be even harder to bear if I didn't have Nellie and John by my side. Henry and Angus are as good as gold, and they are all a great comfort to me. How sad it is to remember Baby Christy Ann, who would now have been five had she not been taken from us at only six months. Everyone has been very kind since you left, and I have particularly valued having such good friends in Dorothy Makinson and Jennie Spellman. Angus had appendicitis during the summer, and the company doctor took great care of him and did the operation. I am very grateful and not so sure we would have received such attention back home in Aspull. I would have found it difficult to cope since you left had it not been for Ellen working for the past four months on the coal screening with the other pit brow girls. She finds it very hard but never complains.

With all my love,
Forever yours,
Elizabeth x

The following morning after breakfast, Sar'nt MacKay called them to attention as the platoon commander entered the hut. They all stood at the end of their beds, and Lieutenant McIvor stood in the centre of the room.

"I have just come from a further briefing by the company commander. I can now tell you that tomorrow afternoon you must be prepared to leave Witley. You will be moved by road transport to Folkestone Harbour and, from there by sea to Boulogne.

"This is the last time I will be addressing you as platoon commander, as I've been posted to 3 Brigade HQ, and I will be leaving first thing tomorrow morning. My replacement is Mr Bell, who I believe some of you already know and who arrives tomorrow. There have been a number of changes in recent times, and I know that the latest platoon organisation chart will be on the company notice board later. Sar'nt MacKay has a copy, which he is going to display in here when we've finished. I wish you all the best of luck in France. I can't say where, but you'll know that soon enough. So, I leave you in the very capable hands of Sar'nt MacKay. Carry on." With that, he saluted, turned, and left the room.

Everyone started talking at once. It seemed like a long time had passed since there had been any news. The platoon sar'nt pinned the notice on the back of the door and then left them to talk excitedly about the developments.

The platoon organisation chart read:

25 Bn Bravo Company 6 Platoon		
OC Lt K Bell		
Pl Sergeant—Sgt MacKay		
No 1 Rifle Section	No 2 Rifle Section	Machine Gunners
Cpl Galbraith	L/Cpl Gregory	L/Cpl MacPherson
Pte Mathers	Pte Heffernan	Pte Walmsley
Pte Clarke	Pte Makinson	Pte Nicholson
Pte Shepherd	Pte Spellman	Pte James
Pte Martin	Pte Hodson	
Pte Hughes	Pte Trenchard	
Pte Morgan	Pte House	
Pte Roberts	Pte Hopewell	
Pte Burns	Pte O'Connor	
Pte Blunt	Pte Kelly	

The rest of the day was spent cleaning and packing equipment ready for the move. And that evening they were all in bed just after last post.

The following morning, whereas William's body clock would normally have meant that he would wake just before reveille, this morning he was awake even earlier than usual to the sound of distant thunder. *A storm is brewing and headed this way no doubt*, he decided.

However, after about ten minutes, the thunder had not receded and seemed to be at more or less the same distance away from Witley than before.

It wasn't until two days later that someone Jimmy had been speaking to at breakfast told him that on the morning of 9 April the "thunder" was in fact the detonation of mines under the advance German trenches, marking the start of the Battle of Vimy Ridge. Apparently, even the prime minister had heard it in London.

The following day was very busy, cleaning and packing equipment before handing it all back into the QM's store. By last post, they were all ready to move off in the morning after breakfast.

CHAPTER 10

U-Boat Threat

THE WHOLE COMPANY was assembled on the square at 1030 hours, and a convoy of twelve trucks arrived shortly afterwards. With everyone loaded by 1100 they left Witley Camp for the last time.

They were to travel by minor roads to Folkestone Harbour and from there by ship to Boulogne.

Having stopped a couple of times on the way, they eventually arrived at the dockside at half past four. The CSM and Sar'nt MacKay went to each vehicle in turn and ordered, "Get yourselves and your kit down and form up by platoon facing the ship named SS *Basil*, then stand easy while we wait for further instructions when Lieutenant Bell returns from the company commander's briefing."

A few minutes later, the CSM appeared and spoke at length with Sar'nt MacKay. There was a lot of nodding and pointing at the ship. Then he came back to speak to John Galbraith and William. "We're going to be here a while. How long, I haven't a clue, so you'd better make yourselves as comfortable as possible in the meantime. The one thing I do know is that when we get the word to move we will follow on immediately after the advance party of the Sherwood Foresters in front."

A further hour passed with no sign of movement to their right at company HQ or the Sherwood Foresters. Although they were well used to standing in the open for hours on end, to add to their discomfort there was a sudden crack of thunder followed by a flash of lightning. Two minutes later, it started to rain quite heavily.

Even with the protection provided by their groundsheets, their legs and feet were feeling the cold and damp. That, together with the lack of food and drink, ensured everyone was feeling pretty miserable.

It was now over two hours since they'd arrived in Folkestone. "I wonder how much longer we're going to be kept waiting, William? I haven't seen Sar'nt MacKay for a good while, and the platoon commander disappeared ages ago. So, there's no one around to ask."

"Well, particularly since it's dark now, it's bound

to make things more difficult Jimmy. By the way, have you seen anything of Peter Spellman? He seems to have gone missing."

"No. Come to think of it, I haven't seen him for a good while William. Do you think he might have gone off and found a pub?"

"I really hope not Jimmy. We shouldn't jump to conclusions so quickly. In fact look, here he comes now."

Peter reappeared, together with a very tall, thin young man wearing overalls.

"Where on earth have you been Pete?" asked Jimmy.

"I met young Ken here in the workshops a bit farther on from here. His best friend is in the QM's store, and I've bought enough rum for everyone in the platoon to have a tot. It'll warm us all up."

Just in time, Sar'nt MacKay reappeared and had overheard the story about the rum. "Well Spellman, I heard that. It's very enterprising of you, and for once, I'm going to turn a blind eye to your absence. At least you've returned sober. Don't try it again, or you'll seriously regret it."

The tot of rum and the fact that the rain had stopped seemed to cheer everyone up, as they all started talking again.

Both William and Jimmy lit their pipes, feeling a little more relaxed. "Pete to the rescue again then William."

"I don't know how he does it Jimmy, but thank God he does."

Although the rain had stopped, in the dark and it was hard to see anything happening nearer to the front of the queue of waiting troops. And it was nearly half past seven o'clock before they were called forward to follow in line behind the Sherwood Foresters.

Once on board the platoon commander came to speak to them. The platoon sar'nt called them to attention.

"Stand the men easy Sar'nt MacKay. Before we set sail you should know that the Germans have deployed large numbers of U-boats in British waters and that the channel is particularly at risk from enemy torpedoes. So, while we're hopeful that the crossing to Boulogne will be trouble free we must be prepared for any eventuality. Are there any questions?"

"Couldn't be clearer sir," Sar'nt MacKay responded. He had been perfectly clear about the risky nature of the crossing, and there were no questions.

Once they had settled, William gathered the

men of 2 Section around him. "Well, boys, this is different—wet clothes; hungry; just too much kit to carry; sat on our kit bags on *Basil* crossing the channel; and, at the same time, the risk of being sunk by a German U-boat. What more could you ask for? Still, we mustn't complain. Tomorrow we'll be ashore in France."

Boulogne

It was late afternoon before they disembarked and were formed up with their gear on the quayside at Boulogne. The dockyard was a scene of frenzied activity as stores and troops were unloaded before dusk settled in and the light failed altogether.

Sar'nt MacKay called the section leaders aside. "If you're ready now, we can go. We're off to a place called Locre, about two hours away by train. Mr Bell tells me we may be there for up to a week or more and that we'll have a couple of days to get settled before 5 Brigade calls on the battalion to provide support, then we could get to see some action. Pass the word on to your men."

"What is this place then Sar'nt?" William asked.

"I've been there before when it was known as Derry Huts. In the main it was used as a transit camp. If I remember, the accommodation is in the good old bell tents, and the food was good on the whole. It's expected that we'll join the battalion in a few days."

Peter Spellman raised his hand. "And this Locre place Sar'nt? Will we have any free time to get familiar with the town and surrounding area?"

Sar'nt MacKay's face reddened. Pete really had pushed things too far this time. "Trust you to ask a bloody stupid question like that Spellman, this is the real thing now. And before you get any other ideas, we will be based near the main assembly area outside a small village south-east of Ypres. And no, there will not be any time for you to be wandering off and getting familiar with anything or anyone. Civilian areas are strictly out of bounds. That is, unless they're occupied by the Germans—when I would definitely encourage you to get in close contact. And I'm sure they will have a warm welcome waiting for you.

"Now back to business. Corporal Galbraith will issue you with twenty rounds of ammunition each. Keep it in your ammo pouch until we get to Locre."

After the short march to the station they joined the end of a long queue of troops waiting for the train. William called over to John Galbraith, "Where are all these going then John? There must be at least two hundred here."

"I understand they're all bound for Locre, William—including the nurses. The rest are reinforcements for different units at the front."

The train was already alongside the platform, and there was just enough room in the last compartment for the 2 Platoon men to squeeze onto the wooden bench seats.

Once the train was clear of the outskirts of the city, William was shocked to see that the countryside and villages they passed through were for the most part a scene of total devastation, with hardly a tree standing or building left intact.

CHAPTER 11

Locre

THE JOURNEY TO Locre took four hours. Once they had collected their equipment, they followed the CSM and company clerk out into a large yard already full of other troops and vehicles being loaded with equipment.

The overall level of noise arising from all this activity, the picture of hundreds of troops for the moment all looking quite bewildered, and the multitude of orders being barked out at the same time was quite overwhelming. William laughed and turned to Jimmy, "Can you hear all that? Utter chaos. I wouldn't be surprised if most of them are following the wrong orders."

No sooner had he spoken than they were brought to their senses with the arrival of Sar'nt MacKay. "Now 6 Platoon, pay attention. From now on you will have one round up the spout at all times. Be prepared, because you never know what's around the next corner. Corporal Galbraith, you will check every man's weapon before we march off. We will be following Alpha Company. The battalion main party has been here since early morning."

"The large body of troops in front of Alpha, Sar'nt—the ones wearing the kilt—they look almost battalion strength to me. Do you know who they are?"

The platoon sar'nt moved nearer to Jimmy "Bound for the Scottish 51st Division I believe, Argyll and Sutherlands. They suffered very heavy casualties at the Ancre—hence the need for such a large reinforcement. I assume you were all told about the history of our association with the Highlanders when you joined the Regiment at Broughton? It's this connection that led to our wearing the Black Watch tartan."

Having loaded their rifles, they picked up the rest of their equipment ready to march off, waiting for Sar'nt MacKay's orders. They didn't have to wait long, "In single file, quick march."

Back in Boulogne William had felt overawed by the numbers boarding the train for Locre, however when they now marched out of the yard and did a right turn into the road he couldn't believe his eyes. As far as the eye could see in the fields on the left side of the road there was row upon row of tents. About every two hundred yards or so there was a sign and an MP sentry guiding the marching troops into their allotted battalion accommodation. On the right-hand side, the fields were full of parked motor vehicles and artillery of every shape and size.

After about five minutes Sar'nt MacKay halted the platoon and cupped a hand to his ear.

"What are we listening for Sar'nt?" asked Trenchard.

"Ssshh. Listen, watch, and learn."

In the distance there was what sounded like a rumble of thunder. But as it had turned out to be an unusually sunny day, a storm was furthest from anyone's mind. Nevertheless, the thunder-like rumbling seemed to grow nearer.

Having gotten away with one interruption, Trenchard tried his luck a second time. "What's that sign MGC for Sar'nt?"

"Machine Gun Corps. I did my training with them on the Lewis and Vickers guns." This time it was Corporal Galbraith who answered.

Sar'nt MacKay frowned. He didn't take kindly to being interrupted, "Nothing to do with machine guns. Look over the field to your front now." He pointed across the road in the direction of the rumbling.

There was a collective intake of breath as they all caught their first sight of a tank, and it was heading in their direction. No doubt the crew was well aware of the same impression their armoured vehicle had on the average foot soldier, whether Allied or enemy; of course, it very much depended upon which direction the tank was travelling at the time.

Thankfully today it stopped about ten yards short of the fence.

"I told you to watch and learn, and eventually now you have."

It must have been another two miles up the road when Sar'nt MacKay stopped before a sign on the left and read out loud for everyone's benefit, "25th (MacKenzie Battalion)."

The MP on duty waved them forward, with 1 Section leading and then William and 2 Section next, followed by the machine gunners and then finally the bombers.

They turned right at a sign that read "Bravo Company Lines". Then eventually, they came to the third row in on the left, marked "6 Platoon".

As they were getting themselves organised, the platoon sar'nt came into the 2 Section tent. "I have some good news for you, boys. As we're now officially on active service, each platoon is entitled to a rum ration of a gallon jar each and every week. And out of that each man gets a tot every morning at stand-to and another one every evening when you are stood down."

"That does sound like really good news," Pete just couldn't resist it.

"I've got a chit here to take to the quartermaster's compound for 'one-gallon jar SRD.' Spellman, you can help collect the first week's ration. I will be personally responsible for the rum jar, you will be helping me issue the ration."

Despite their past history, Sar'nt MacKay and Peter Spellman seemed to get on surprisingly well together when it came to the safekeeping and distribution of the rum ration. In fact, this worked so well that after two weeks. Pete was put in total charge of organising this critical supply—an appointment obviously welcomed by William and the other Wigan pals.

The Spellman Singalong

On the second day at Locre, Jimmy and Peter cornered William when there appeared to be no one else around. "How's things with you, William?"

"Okay, I suppose, Jimmy. What can I do for you?"

"Well, Pete here has an idea about what we should do with the rum ration for the non-drinkers in the platoon."

"It had never occurred to me before that there might be any who don't drink Jimmy. So, what's your idea then Pete?"

"Soon after starting the rum round, I found out that there are about five Willum, and they just gave their rum ration away. So, I thought that if I saved the spare rations I could sell them to drinkers for fifty cents each. And in that way, the non-drinkers at least got something in return, like extra tobacco or cigarettes."

"That's a great idea Pete. I'll put it to John Galbraith as No. 1 Section leader, and if he agrees, then we should do it."

John agreed. So from the second night at Locre when he called at the other tents, Pete bought the surplus rum from the non-drinkers. Then later back in 2 Section tent he sold the extra tots to the eager drinkers who were only too delighted to get their hands on double the regular ration.

Had they known, the officers would no doubt have disapproved of such a practice, whilst Sar'nt MacKay, on the other hand, positively encouraged it, and at the same time making sure no one had more than a double issue. In any case, he enjoyed his rum tipple as much as the next man.

Happily sipping their extra rum, as the evening

wore on the atmosphere in 2 Section tent became increasingly relaxed, and in the hour before last post Pete entertained the section and most of the rest of the platoon by playing his mouth organ and leading a singalong. His repertoire seemed to have no limits, and although they knew the chorus lines, few knew many of the verses.

However, Peter could remember them all, and among the tunes most favoured by everyone were, "I Don't Want to Be a Soldier", "Pack Up Your Troubles", "It's a Long Way to Tipperary", "Keep the Home Fires Burning", and "Goodbye Dolly Gray."

The regulars at the singalong were more than happy with this arrangement, while those with the fifty-cent-a-tot reward collected a few extra dollars over the week, which made them all equally content.

On Saturday just after last post, William was sat outside with his last pipe when Jimmy came out of the tent to light his, "I thought I'd join you over a smoke."

"Well it's a nice enough evening Jimmy, so sit yourself here next to me. I thought Pete kept everyone smiling again tonight?"

"As usual, he always does. Always good for a laugh, our Pete."

CHAPTER 12

A Game of Chess

DURING THE FIRST weekend of June, the battalion left Locre and moved by road to the corps reserve area near Gouy-Servins, where they were to provide support for 5 Brigade recce patrols for three weeks.

The facility at Gouy had originally been set up as a resupply depot. It included the Canadian hospital and then further extended to its present size, allowing sufficient space for units passing through on their way to the front.

They had been allotted hutted accommodation, and were in the middle of unpacking stores and equipment when Sar'nt MacKay came into the 6 Platoon hut with the news that the whole battalion had to assemble on the drill square at 1100 hours to be addressed by the commanding officer.

It was nearly midday when the CO, 2IC, and the adjutant arrived. "I have news of immense importance affecting us all, and it is a question of good news and sad news. The good news is that with immediate effect the Canadian Corps is to be commanded by a Canadian for the first time. Lieutenant General Sir Arthur Currie, who as commander of the 1st Division played such an important part in the success at Vimy Ridge, will take the charge. I don't doubt for one moment that the corps will continue to achieve even greater success in future. The sad news is that of course, we lose General Byng who has been promoted to head the Third Army."

The battalion ranks fell silent for a few moments, while everyone considered whether these moves would actually affect them in any way.

The CO then continued, "I don't expect our operations to be affected over the next few months, other than you are likely to be moved several times in the coming weeks. I like to compare this to a game of chess—gradually moving the pieces towards the end objective, and hopefully, checkmate. But more about this in due course."

The battalion was then dismissed, and companies marched back to their accommodation. Sar'nt MacKay had been chatting to the CSM on their way back and followed the platoon into the hut. "Well, other than the news of generals being promoted, we're not sure what to make of all that except that we are likely to be moved a number of times in the coming weeks. Right, let's carry on sorting the equipment."

The period at Gouy was relatively quiet, and the only event of note during the first two weeks was the brigade sports day at the Chateau de la Haie, notable mainly for the fact that the 25th Battalion failed to excel in most competitions, other than Kelly from the platoon who came second in the high jump. The most successful athletes all seemed to belong to the 24th.

A further week passed with still no call from 5 Brigade for patrolling duties, until on the third Sunday Sar'nt MacKay took the chance to visit other platoons at the same time that Peter Spellman did his rum rounds. This gave him the chance to call on CSM Haylett at company HQ, then he came back with Pete to tell everyone what he had heard.

"Here's my understanding regarding the battalion's next moves. It's all a bit vague at the moment, and although the CO probably knows where we're going from here, he couldn't possibly know what the end game is. That's for the generals to decide, so really, I'm none the wiser. Sorry, chaps."

After breakfast on the following Thursday, they

were all back in the hut changing for a short run around the camp perimeter when Sar'nt MacKay and the CSM appeared. "Brigade needs six men to give cover for a patrol by Recce tonight, leaving here at 1230 hours and returning early tomorrow morning. So I need three volunteers each from 1 and 2 Sections. Corporal Gregory, you should definitely go, to keep the others steady."

After some debate, William handed a piece of paper to Sar'nt MacKay, who read the names for the sar'nt major. "Corporal Gregory, then Martin, Heffernan, Kelly, Makinson, and Spellman—a good mix of experience and youth I'd say."

As the time to leave on the patrol drew nearer, the atmosphere in the hut was tense, particularly as this was the first time that 6 Platoon was likely to see some action.

At a quarter past eleven, Sar'nt MacKay carried out a final check of the patrol's rifles and ammunition. And at 1215 hours a four-by-four Chevrolet pulled up in the road outside. William then checked the men onto the back of the vehicle, and they moved off.

After they had been underway for about ten minutes, it was noticeable that no one had spoken since leaving. All were preoccupied with their own thoughts. The only sound was from the vehicle's engine.

Peter was the first to speak. "Any idea where we're headed Willum?"

"Not a clue Pete. But I guess we'll soon know."

After travelling along several typically long, straight roads for over an hour, the truck slowed and then stopped by the side of the road. William looked out, and there was nothing much to be seen on either side. "Stay where you are for the moment while I speak to the driver and see what he knows."

William jumped down and spoke to the driver, who stayed in his cab. "Where are we, driver? And what happens now?"

"I've been here a few times before. It's one of many dropping off points for these scouting patrols. A couple of hundred yards further on there's a crossroads, and to the left is a small place called Bois-Grenay. Not much to be seen there. Then either straight over or to the right are the areas where the Germans leave their front line and despatch their patrols, much as we're doing now."

Just as the driver had finished speaking, a second vehicle drew up behind. An officer got out of the cab and came over to William, "You must be Corporal Gregory I take it? Captain Forsyth."

William saluted, the officer returned the salute and at the same time shook William's hand and then continued "Right, Corporal, we'll split into two patrols—six each. I'll be going straight ahead with Corporals Simpson and Jackman from Brigade Recce, together with the three from your team, while the second patrol, led by Sar'nt Beatty from Brigade staff, including your support, will go right at the crossroads, then after about two miles you will be turning left across the field, where you can see what used to be a small copse on the far ridge. We've been there before. With my patrol, I'll loop round in a long pincer movement until we meet up with you again at the copse."

"Has there been much action in the area recently sir?"

"Not so much in the immediate area, but almost continuous shelling in the areas of Lille and Festubert, with scouting patrols and occasional skirmishing from the direction we're interested in this evening. After the recent major shows earlier in the year, Fritz has tended to regroup to the west of Vimy and in the area of Loos/Lens. But it's their preparations for a further thrust towards Ypres where our interests are focussed tonight."

"Roger, sir," William replied. "As our commanding

officer said recently, it's all the same as a game of chess. I suggest Spellman, Kelly, and Heffernan go with you, sir. Makinson and Martin will go with me and the rest from your team."

"Excellent we're all set then. We'll lead the observation, and I need your men to give cover when needed."

Both patrols then set off and went their separate ways at the crossroads. The terrain was typical of the region, consisting of the seemingly never-ending straight roads, with very little in the way of trees or the occasional ruined farm building on either side. By now, the light was fading fast.

William's patrol had covered about two miles when Sar'nt Beatty lifted his arm for a stop and then signalled left across a field. They jumped across the roadside ditch, and then slowly made their way towards the far side until they reached a slight ridge and the sparse cover offered by the remains of what used to be a small copse.

They all took up positions lying low between the scrub and broken tree stumps. After settling in for about half an hour the patrol leader pointed across the field to the north-west, and in the failing light, William could just about see some movement about

200 yards away. He leaned over and nudged Jimmy, who nodded to confirm he'd also seen the activity.

Although it couldn't have been more than five minutes, but seemed much longer, William could hear low voices approaching—definitely German. All six members of the patrol held their breath and readied themselves to spring into action. The voices, although muted, were nevertheless getting much nearer and then much louder. William could just pick up bits of conversation—something like, "Kanadische patrouillen," and then "Hier Hans."

William held his breath, not daring to make any noise. Then he felt as though he was about to sneeze, but didn't.

Fritz continued talking, by now it wasn't as clear and appeared to be moving away. There must have been at least two of them, most probably more, and they had walked straight past six Canadians hugging the ground closely. It helped of course that it was now dark.

They lay there for about another twenty minutes or so and then carefully got to their feet. Sar'nt Beatty pointed back across the field towards the roadside ditch they had crossed earlier. They set off in single file, trying the keep any noise to the minimum. It took them nearly half an hour to reach the ditch.

At the ditch they stopped for a moment to catch their breath. When Jimmy turned towards William, his eyes were all that was visible in the dark, "That was a close thing William."

Suddenly a flare from the direction of the copse lit the sky, followed by a burst of fire from the Germans' LMG. The MG08 was the equivalent of the British Lewis gun. Corporal Simpson's knees folded under him, and he fell forward flat on his face.

Instinctively all five went down on one knee, training their rifles back towards the copse. They all shuffled backwards on their bellies into the waist-deep ditch. William fired three rounds in quick succession, and the others followed suit. At the same time, the air was filled with return fire from the German position.

Martin, who was the patrol's nominated medical orderly, crawled out of the ditch towards Corporal Simpson's prone body.

"Martin, get back here!" William called, but of course there was no chance he could hear.

The exchanges continued on and off for a full ten minutes. The rate of fire from William and the others in the ditch slowed to something like two rounds a minute, and in the case of Sar'nt Beatty, stopped altogether. He was now completely out of ammunition.

Martin quickly realised the seriousness of the situation and crawled back into the ditch with a full ammunition pouch, presumably Corporal Simpson's. William grabbed the pouch and lying on his side handed five to each of the others. Turning first of all to Jimmy who was lying immediately behind, he passed five rounds into his outstretched hand. Then twisting to his front again, he looked at Martin, Sar'nt Beatty, and Corporal Jackman, who were crouching closely together.

Eager to get their hands on this desperately needed resupply, they stretched their arms towards William, slightly raising their profiles just at the moment the Germans raked the ditch with another long burst of fire LMG. All three were hit and fell in a heap, with Martin falling face to face with William, spewing his choking blood everywhere. William managed to roll him on his side and wiped the blood from his face with the back of his hand. Jimmy was half-buried in debris from the collapsed sides of the ditch.

As his head began to clear, his first thoughts were that they would either be the next to be killed or would be taken prisoner. Once more, he recalled Major Macleod's warning and wondered was being taken prisoner by the Hun really a fate worse than death?

The position now seemed utterly hopeless. They were the only ones from the patrol left alive.

For the next few minutes, all was quiet. Then fresh flares lit the sky, followed by a number of explosions and more small arms fire but none coming in their direction. Then quiet descended on the field, and the only sounds came from artillery exchanges nearer to Loos to the south and south-west towards Festubert.

William turned and stared open-mouthed at Jimmy. Both were stunned, not fully comprehending what was happening.

Then the silence was broken as a now familiar voice called out, "Sar'nt Beatty, Corporal Gregory, we're coming across now."

It was Captain Forsyth. "Corporal Gregory here, sir," William replied.

Captain Forsyth appeared and crouched down on the edge of the ditch, shaking his head, despairing at the scene of devastation below him. He called over his shoulder, "Sar'nt Beatty's gone I'm afraid, Corporal MacPhee. Bring Kelly and Heffernan down here. There are four dead. I want you to move them up top, where they can be picked up later. Spellman, you come take a look at Corporal Gregory and Makinson. Clean them up as best you can and see if they have any wounds that need dressing."

William was still quite dazed when he looked up to see what he thought was a familiar figure staring down at him. "Peter, is that you?"

"Yes, it's me all right, Willum. You're in a right old state. Blood everywhere. Where were you hit? Where's the pain?"

"I don't think I was wounded Pete, so any blood must be Martin's. He fell on top of me. I'm okay now."

"That's good, Willum. Jimmy's escaped without harm as well. Right. Let's get you cleaned up."

William was straining to focus clearly on Peter. "What on earth's that you've got on your head?"

"We bumped into a much larger German patrol on the opposite side of the road Willum. We opened fire the moment they appeared. And although we were well outnumbered, luckily the recce boys had a Lewis gun, and in the end we killed nearly a dozen Hun. We took two prisoners, and one of them was an officer wearing this helmet. They call it a pickelhaube."

Jimmy was now pretty well recovered and was

listening closely to Pete's story. "So what are you doing with it Pete?"

"Captain Forsyth ordered the prisoners to empty their pockets and stand with their backs against what was left of a wall. They were sure we were going to shoot them where they stood. Poking my rifle to the officer's chest, I persuaded him to donate the helmet and his Mauser pistol.

"I thought we could stick the helmet spike in the ground and pee in it instead of a bucket Willum."

"That's a really good idea Peter. I think."

"Here's the pistol Willum. It's for you. I checked and it has a full magazine."

"Thanks Peter. That'll come in handy one of these days. Fits neatly into the side pocket of my jacket."

Cité Saint-Pierre

The summer weather so far had been consistently warm and dry—probably the best in these first three years of the war. However, today Sod's Law prevailed, and the sky at daybreak had been overcast with a persistent light drizzle, now late morning it turned to a steady downpour.

For the past half hour the platoon had been formed up on the road outside the hut ready for the march towards Cité St-Pierre. Sar'nt MacKay locked the door then turned his attention to the groundsheet-clad men, "This is the first time in a long while you've needed to wear your groundsheets. With your reversed rifles slung underneath, make sure you hold on tightly throughout the move, as we don't want any rust anywhere, do we?"

"No Sar'nt," they all replied.

"I've just got to hand in the keys to the HQ office on our way out, then we'll be on our way along the Noulette to Liévin road and on to Cité St-Pierre on the outskirts of Lens. That's where we take over trenches from the 24th Battalion."

"They've been there for three weeks, whereas I understand we'll be there for no longer than two or three days until we're relieved by the 21st. Right you miserable-looking lot, left turn, quick march."

Five minutes later, they were brought to a halt on the drill square, joining numbers 1 and 3 Platoons.

This was the first occasion everyone had seen Major Wainwright riding his horse, recently shipped over from his father's estate in Hampshire. The CSM called the company to attention. "Fine weather for ducks, eh, me boys? Now pay attention to the company commander."

"It's a shame about the awful weather. But then

war is more often than not fought in bad weather.
Before we set off, I wanted to introduce you to my
horse Cicero who is a four-year-old named after a
famous winner of the derby. Of course, most of you
already know my Jack Russell Toby, who, by the way
is six. Wherever we go from now on you will see rats,
which are almost impossible to control. However
much you might be tempted, under no circumstances
are you to waste valuable ammunition on the vermin.
Now that we have Toby on board, I plan to lend his
services to each platoon in turn for two days at a
time. He is by far the best ratter I've ever seen, and
he will do his best to keep the rat population at a
manageable level wherever you are, be it in trenches
or the ruins of buildings. I'm sure you will devise
your own methods of dealing with those left after
Toby moves on. In the meantime, I wish you all the
very best of luck. So let us get on with the fun and
games. Sar'nt Major, carry on."

With Toby alongside, the company commander
turned Cicero towards the road, followed by the
Platoon Sar'nts calling out the time. As was often
the case, William and 2 Section brought up the tail
end of the marching column.

After nearly an hour the rain showed no sign
of easing, and even Toby was looking miserable in

these conditions. He didn't enjoy being so cold and wet. Trudging along what had once been a road but was now flooded in parts and becoming increasingly muddy made the going underfoot quite treacherous. Bringing up the rear and following in the footsteps of the rest of the company, most of the men in the section including William, slipped and stumbled many times, and some lost their balance altogether, falling in the mud and having to be helped back onto their feet. Hampered by these worsening conditions, progress was extremely slow, with frequent stops to restore some semblance of order in the ranks.

Eventually the column halted just before midnight. And nearly half an hour later, word was passed back that Major Wainwright had been stopped by a patrol from the Brigade Recce company. Although the conditions had worsened considerably since they set out, it was at least an opportunity for William and a chosen few in the platoon to enjoy a welcome swig of rum from Spellman's emergency supply. Jimmy turned to William, "I hope this means we're nearly there now. Brigade Recce, eh? That probably means one of two things; either there's trouble waiting for us up ahead, or we're lost, which do you think, William?"

After a brief hesitation Jimmy answered his own

question, "But hopefully they're simply guiding us in. Although my groundsheet is keeping me dry from the waist up, I feel the damp all over, and my legs and puttees are soaked through to the skin. You must be the same William. The sooner we find some proper shelter the better."

Doing his best to raise a smile, William nodded in reply, "I bet the company commander regrets his decision to set out on horseback. He's finding it hard going—the horse I mean."

As they were speaking, Mr Bell came back from the front of the line and stood next to Sar'nt MacKay. William could clearly hear the conversation.

"We are just outside St-Pierre, and thank goodness the rain has eased off for the time being. The Brigade Recce boys will be leading us into the Norfolk trench system. The 24th has been in there for the past three weeks, and I understand they've been pretty badly beaten up by the German whizz-bangs and gas. We must be through the communication trench and settled into Norfolk Alpha before dawn. Hopefully the rain will hold off until then. Any questions?"

As if in reply, there was a flash of lightning overhead, followed by a loud clap of thunder, and the steady rain returned, only much heavier than before.

William shouted, hoping to be heard above the noise of the pouring rain, "What's the position now with the Hun facing the Norfolk trench?"

"They're not causing too many problems right now. But exactly where and in what numbers, we're not sure. They seem to be constantly on the move, just as we are. Right then. We'd better get moving."

About a quarter of an hour later, when the column next halted, Sar'nt MacKay came back with the latest news, "The Norfolk Communication Trench is only about a hundred yards farther on, and there are guides there to point the way into Alpha. Lieutenant Bell is already in situ. The 24th guys are already moving out, and our immediate task is to get in there, post sentries, and set up a Lewis gun at either end of the trench to cover the buildings opposite."

At the entrance to Norfolk, there was a step down into the trench, which had several inches of standing rainwater overflowing the duckboards, deeper in parts than others, and this made it slow going for everyone. Tucker was there to lead the way in, and five minutes later they saw Mr Bell standing next to a wooden sign freshly marked "6 Pl".

Andrew and 1 Section were the first to take over sentry duty. Meanwhile, everyone else set to work clearing up as much of the mess as possible, storing packs and ammunition, as well as what little food rations were left.

Alpha trench was about twenty feet long and about five feet wide, and the high sandbagged walls were well made and boarded in sections. The duckboards were overflowing with stagnant water, and at the far end, there were no duckboards, just a pool of water. William tested the depth of water with his stick. It must have been at least two feet deep, "Real deathtrap that, for sure. One foot wrong or too much rum, particularly on a dark night."

Jimmy edged a little nearer to get a closer look, "The stench makes me want to throw up. I don't think they spent much time digging a latrine. Goodness only knows how they managed."

William nodded in agreement. "We're relatively clean compared with this lot. At least we've got Peter's Pickelhaube to pee in. The whole damned place stinks, but there's little we can do about it at the moment. We're going to have one helluva job keeping ourselves clean and dry in all this mess. I don't know how big the dugout is, but maybe we could take it in turns sharing it with Lieutenant Bell?"

Sar'nt MacKay came to the dugout entrance. "What do you think, Sar'nt?" William asked.

"When I looked into the dugout just now, it's pretty roomy compared with many I've seen. There are blankets hung from the roof separating an area for Mr Bell on the one side and six wooden benches on the other for those not on duty. So yes, whenever possible, there will be somewhere to clean up and get some rest. By the way, we've already asked company HQ to send a runner with a request for a new supply of duckboards from the Quartermaster."

Fortunately, by daybreak the rain had stopped altogether. There had been no sign of the enemy, nor was there any word from the rear echelon regarding when the extra duckboards might be delivered. It wasn't until late morning when two men arrived carrying large backpacks, "More rations and ammunition for 6 Platoon."

"Is that all?" asked Sar'nt MacKay. "I was told that a runner arrived yesterday and delivered a requisition to the Quartermaster's compound. Apparently after leaving, he'd covered no more than two hundred yards when he was felled by a stray bullet from an exchange of fire between D Company and the German lines. The storeman said that in any case it was all a waste of time, as there were no spare duckboards in stock."

"Nothing surprises me any longer. Anyway, your

delivery of both food and ammunition is very welcome. Too often recently, it's only been ammunition."

Pete Spellman was obviously very happy seeing the ration boxes, as despite his being the smallest man in the platoon, he always seemed to be the most desperately hungry. "I don't know who it was that said an army marches on its stomach. Well not in this damned army it doesn't!"

Jimmy smiled and nodded in agreement. "However, we must be grateful for whatever we get, Pete. Some poor blighters may have nothing to eat."

There was now enough bread for a loaf to each section, some cheese, and a half dozen tins of bully beef to share among the platoon. Together with the rum ration it made for a quite acceptable meal. There was no word as to when they might expect a further delivery of rations. The men of 1 Section ate their food first before they took watch at the wall from William's section.

Just after midday, the Germans opposite opened fire with their trench mortars and heavy machine guns. The firing was pretty indiscriminate, and other than flying debris falling into the trench, there was no harm done. In fact, there were no reported injuries in the whole company.

It did, however, give Corporal Galbraith and

his men the chance to exercise their Lewis guns in return. And although these sporadic bursts of fire probably caused little damage, the exchanges were quite deafening.

There hadn't been much free time for letter writing since leaving the United Kingdom, and William hadn't even found the time to read the latest letter from Elizabeth; but now with nearly two hours in the dugout until the next spell on sentry, William opened the envelope:

38 Argyll Street
Glace Bay, NS
18 June 1917

Dearest William,

We are all hoping and praying that this letter finds you safe and in good health. I'm sorry that it is a short note, but young Angus has been very poorly and has only yesterday got home from hospital after having had his appendix removed. The company doctor has been wonderful, and the nursing staff at the hospital looked after him very well. I couldn't have asked for more. The other children are fine and growing up so quickly.

I did have some sad news from home, when last week I was surprised to receive a letter from your Bertha to say that Bea Hardacre has died. She caught pneumonia a second time and passed away at home in early May sometime. She was sixty-six.

Bertha also said that your mam, dad, and everyone else are all doing well.

That's all for now

Always yours, my love,
Elizabeth x

There wasn't enough time right now to reply. But Elizabeth's letter was yet another with a mix of the good news about Angus, and bad news about poor Bea, who after all had been so intimately involved in helping with his own birth some thirty-eight years ago.

With no time to dwell on this news, he re-joined the others, who were busy cleaning their weapons and then as best they could, themselves. As part of the personal hygiene routine, they generally took the time to shave. Then, turning their long johns and shirts inside out, burning the lice off with a lighted candle or a cigarette before putting them back on again, and of course at the same time changing their socks.

William's thoughts then returned to the question of the missing duckboards and the deep pool of water outside. So he got Jimmy and Jack Hodson to help tie a length of rope across the end of the trench and then draped an old vest over to act as a warning to anyone tempted to step out as far as the end.

CHAPTER 13

Three Flashes

IT WAS APPROACHING two o'clock in the morning of what was to be their first full day near St-Pierre, and William was looking forward to a couple of hours rest when 1 Section took over at 0300. This had been their third stint at the trench wall since they arrived.

Much earlier, soon after dark, the mortar platoon had fired several phosphorus bombs into the ruined buildings opposite. This had started a large fire, providing extra illumination across no man's land, and there was still a dim light thrown on the scene from the dying embers.

There had been no reaction from the Germans, casting further doubt on whether they were even still there. Or perhaps some had been deployed to reinforce other units still involved in heavy exchanges of small arms fire to the north-east nearer to Loos.

Peter Spellman and Clarke were each stood on the top rungs of trench ladders, just sufficient for them to lean over and scan no man's land, with William standing farther to their left on the concrete fire step. From there, he was also able to see any sign of movement to their front, and at this time he couldn't hear or see any movement across the way in St-Pierre.

All thoughts of a nice sleep in the relative warmth of the dugout were suddenly interrupted with a tap on his shoulder. Wide awake once more, William turned to find himself facing Major Wainwright, CSM Campbell, Mr Bell, and of course Toby.

The officers had climbed up alongside him and were studying the area towards the buildings directly opposite. "All quiet across there Corporal Gregory?" asked the company sar'nt major.

"Yes sir. No movement. No sign of life other than the damned rats as usual."

Major Wainwright tugged at William's arm again. "Good that there's nothing happening across the way. And as far as the rats are concerned, I promised Mr Bell you could have Toby for two days starting this morning. He'll certainly clear the dugout and this trench for you, although no man's land is too big a task for one little Jack Russell."

"Thanks sir. That's much appreciated."

The major rested his map case by the entrance to the dugout and turned to Toby, pointing at the case he instructed. "Toby, sit. Stay now. Good boy."

Toby obediently lay down, guarding his master's bag.

"It does appear to be perfectly still out there. Just what we wanted, eh, Sar'nt Major?"

The company commander looked knowingly at the CSM and then, with a thin smile, nodded to Lieutenant Bell, "The Sar'nt Major and I are going on a recce over the other side to see what they're doing or even whether there's anyone there at the moment. They do seem to be on the move quite often of late. Anyway, the only way I can think of to signal when we're ready to return without attracting too much attention is that I'll flick my cigarette lighter on and off three times. So you will have to keep your eyes peeled. As soon as I signal, I'll need your section to give cover until we're back here safely. The other platoon commanders have been warned, and while we're gone, Captain McInnis is holding the reins."

"Yes sir," William acknowledged.

Major Wainwright and the CSM climbed up the ladder and quickly disappeared over the top. William resumed his spot on the fire step just in time to catch sight of the backsides of the OC and CSM, now well across no man's land and carefully circling around broken barbed wire obstacles and numerous shell holes, before disappearing among the ruins. There was no reaction from Fritz so William assumed that there was no one there.

It must have been no longer than ten minutes later that the three flashes signalled that they were ready to make it back across. They set off running and must have barely covered a around five yards when a flare illuminated the sky and the Hun machine-gunners further up to what was their left opened fire. Both fell instantly. Their motionless bodies weren't even halfway across no man's land.

This triggered the whole section, including the Lewis guns, to open fire in response. There was no way of knowing whether their fire caused any damage, but after the horror of what they had just witnessed, they felt much better for having loosened off a few rounds. This quite indiscriminate exchange lasted for about ten minutes, then all fell quiet again. Even the rats seemed to have gone into hiding.

William could hear Lieutenant Bell on the phone in the dugout, "Roger. Will do."

A few minutes later, he came out of the dugout

and then crossed to stand next to William, "Just spoken to Captain McInnis and arranged that the other platoons hold fire while the stretcher bearers bring them both back in starting at 0345 hours. That gives them twenty minutes from now to be ready."

"Roger that sir," William replied.

Five minutes later, Munro and James passed along the trench carrying spare magazines for the Lewis guns. Munro climbed the ladder to the right and handed over the ammunition to Corporal Galbraith who was set up just over the top, while James went left to resupply Sid Walmsley with the second gun.

At half past two, flares were put up from Company HQ and immediately the Lewis guns opened fire in the general direction of the Germans at the top far right of no man's land. At the same time the mortar platoon pumped a number of rounds into the ruins of St-Pierre. This provided sufficient cover for the two stretcher-bearer parties to cross and pick up the bodies, returning them to Norfolk Zero from where they were to be moved to the hospital at Gouy-Servins.

At three o'clock, 1 Section took over from William's team. It had been quiet since the bodies of Major Wainwright and CSM Crawford had been recovered. As William stepped down from the fire step he noticed that Toby was still doing his duty lying in front of his master's belongings. "Spellman!" he called out, "Come and look after Toby will you?"

Peter Spellman had only just laid down to get some sleep but got up, picked up the map case, and called Toby, "There's a good boy. You follow me and I'll get you some water."

Despite this major setback, the following morning with B Company now under the temporary command of Captain McInnis, it was business as usual for the rest of the battalion. That meant daily artillery exchanges and snipers on either side responding to any sign of movement.

Three days after the deaths of the company commander and CSM, battalion HQ was hit by prolonged and particularly heavy shelling, including gas. The attack, at the end of the day, resulted in two dead and six quite badly wounded; A week later, 3 Platoon lost four in one shelling attack; Finally 6 Platoon lost Hughes and Nicholson from the bombers' section when they were shot by a German sniper as they were working with Corporal Galbraith strengthening the sandbag defences for the two Lewis guns on top of the trench.

The fifteen-day spell in the trenches at St-Pierre had for most proved to be a bitter pill to swallow, a hard lesson learned about life in the front line. Compared with the rest of the battalion, B Company had got off pretty lightly, having suffered only five dead.

CHAPTER 14

Bouvigny Huts

NOW MID-JULY, the battalion was due to move to Bouvigny Huts as soon as they were relieved by the 26th (New Brunswickers). Before leaving St-Pierre, Sar'nt MacKay was made Bravo Company acting CSM, and Andrew Bowes was promoted to platoon sergeant in his place, Andrew retaining responsibility for 1 Rifle Section.

On the same evening after these promotions, William and Jimmy were in the dugout enjoying a pipe together while waiting for the daily rum ration to be delivered. "Things won't be quite the same now that Sarn't Major MacKay will be spending more time in company HQ as well as with the other platoons."

"That's true William. I'll miss him not breathing down my neck night and day. And Galbraith must be disappointed not to have been made up to platoon sar'nt. What do you think?"

"Payback time for the way he treated the two young lads in the gunners' section I'm sure. CSM MacKay is well satisfied all round with the new set-up."

Peter Spellman had arrived at the end of his rum round and was listening to the comments on the changes. William looked up to see Pete standing just inside the doorway. "Oh, hello there Pete. I didn't see you there. It's a good job we weren't talking about you then! Anyway, you're a sight for sore eyes. Got any extras today?"

"This is all that's left, and there's no guarantee we'll have the same allowance when we move again. So, I think we should share all I have. We'll maybe restart the singalongs when we get to Bouvigny. I think there's enough for a good mug full for each of us. Here you are then." Peter topped up their mugs, and they wished each other good luck.

The following morning was dry and sunny, although quite chilly. They left St-Pierre just after eight o'clock, marching west across country towards Noulette and then off in the direction of the Bouvigny Huts camp. When they stopped for a break, William had a short chat with Andrew Bowes, who of course was now the new platoon sar'nt, "I'm looking forward to the time at the huts Andrew. Everyone is exhausted so the rest will do them a world of good."

"Yes. I agree William. The whole platoon has worked damned hard and they deserve a break."

"I wonder whatever happened to poor Major Wainwright's horse, or for that matter, the groom? I've seen neither hide nor hair of them since the OC was killed."

"I'm not sure," Andrew replied.

"But my guess is that the groom will already be back in the UK. As for Cicero, there's such a shortage of horses he was probably redeployed elsewhere within the division."

"Yes. I'm sure that's what happened Andrew. And as for Toby, he did a great job on the rats in St-Pierre. I saw him with Peter Spellman only this morning."

After the platoon arrived at the huts, Sar'nt Major MacKay and the new company commander carried out a tour of the accommodation to see how everyone was settling in. Major Harrington was a stocky, barrel-chested man, sporting a fine handlebar moustache matching that of the CSM. When they entered the 6 Platoon accommodation, the sar'nt major barked, "Listen up now. Form a semicircle while the company commander speaks."

"Well, we made it to Bouvigny Huts. I thought the march from St-Pierre this morning made a pleasant change for you, what with the good weather and no time pressure, and I'm pleased to see you're settling in here. While I'm here, there are a few matters I want to draw to your attention."

Referring to his notes, Major Harrington continued, "First of all, and needless to say, I was deeply saddened to learn of the deaths of Major Wainwright and CSM Haylett, both fine soldiers and extremely nice men, they will be sadly missed. I was in officer training with Major Wainwright.

"The accommodation and fresh rations here is, to state the obvious, much improved from that which we have been used to. So make the most of your time here to clean up and get some well-earned rest. Towards the end of next month we are to be involved in a major operation closer to Lens, but more about that a little nearer the time.

"From tomorrow morning onwards, the order of dress when on the move will be kilt and balmoral; beret or helmet when in action against the Hun."

The company commander half turned as if to leave and then, smiling, he looked once more to his notes. "Ah, and I almost forgot. I spoke to the commanding officer this afternoon, and there may be a possibility of a forty-eight-hour pass to Abbeyville sometime next week."

This triggered a round of cheering, with a great deal of slapping on the back. The good news seemed to be never-ending.

"Quiet!" the CSM bellowed in his loudest drill square voice.

Order restored, Major Harrington continued. "Finally, I wish you all the best of luck. And I know that, when we come to grips with Fritz again, you will for sure make them rue the day they ever heard of the MacKenzie Battalion, the Fighting 25th."

The company commander turned to leave. "Carry on Sar'nt Major."

Later that evening, having cleaned up and visited the showers, they had a hot meal of cabbage soup followed by potatoes and bully beef. Needless to say, that first night at Bouvigny Huts, they all slept very soundly, and life for now seemed pretty good to the members of Number 6 Platoon. However, both the promised ten-day rest period at the Huts and the prospect of a leave pass to Abbeyville didn't stretch as far as five days, both soon proved to be no more than a fanciful dream.

After the Sunday morning multifaith church service led by the battalion padre, the CSM gathered all those present from B Company to give them the news that they were to be on standby for yet another move the following Wednesday, "Major Harrington will give everyone a briefing once he has all the details. But my understanding is that we will be based back near St-Pierre, even closer to Lens, in the cellars under the cottages in Cité St-Edouard."

The following afternoon was spent on the firing range, and as they were pasting up fresh targets in the butts, Tucker arrived unexpectedly. He spoke to Andrew, who then beckoned Peter Spellman over. After a few brief words, Pete went off with Andrew, presumably to Company HQ.

Having had the live firing disrupted, William organised the platoon into three sections ready for firing practice. But at the back of his mind, he couldn't help wondering what had happened to Peter.

"Do you think there might be trouble 't mill then William?" asked Jimmy.

"We'll soon know, I'm sure," William replied.

About five minutes later Andrew returned to take back control of the firing practice. "Thanks for taking the lead William. Tucker came up with the news that Spellman's grandma has died, and so poor Peter's naturally very upset. I think he's best left alone for the time being."

"I'm sorry to hear that Andrew, I know he was very close to his grandma. She more or less brought him up in his early years. Thank goodness we're here and not at the front. There's never a good time for news like this, but it's certainly better here."

That evening, Pete Spellman was unusually quiet as was to be expected given his news from home earlier. No more rum. No more sing-song.

William called him over, "I'm sorry to hear about your grandma Peter, I understand how you feel. You told me before that she was quite ill, so given time, I hope you'll realise that she's now in a better place and isn't suffering any longer."

"Thanks Willum, it's good to talk. And you're right. She hated sickness all her life."

For the next few days at the huts, the men were blessed with fine weather, which was a welcome bonus. It was such a shame that their stay would turn out to be much shorter than they had originally expected.

CHAPTER 15

Door But No Wall

ON WEDNESDAY AFTERNOON, the whole company was paraded on the square to be addressed by Major Harrington.

"Here we go again then. Another move back to the Lens area, with which of course we are now becoming very familiar. We will reassemble here at 2030 hours tonight and then march the reverse route via Noulette, past St-Pierre, and on much closer to Lens at St-Édouard. There we are to take over from the Princess Patricia's in the cellars under what used to be a row of miners' cottages. It's going to be foggy tonight, so I was somewhat relieved when the CSM assured me that he's made this particular trek so many times he could do it with his eyes closed!"

They set off on time, and after what must have been at least two hours, they were finding it tough going due to the dense fog. Every few yards, William would turn to check that Jimmy was still behind him. "Are you okay Jimmy? Everyone still following you?"

"I'm still here William. Pete and the others are struggling to keep up, but they seem to be managing by holding onto the man in front's pack."

"That's good, all I can see is Morgan's back at the tail end of 1 Section. I only hope that the CSM really does know the way like the back of his hand."

Suddenly, William became aware that Morgan had stopped, so he turned to Jimmy, "Quick Jimmy. Pass the word back to stop and wait."

Then he could hear someone approaching from the front, it was Andrew, "Ah, there you are William. Is everything okay back here?"

"Yes, I suppose so Andrew. But it's not exactly what you would call an enjoyable stroll in the countryside, is it? When I checked with mine a while back they were all still with us, although I don't know about the gunners."

"Well, I do know they're not lost William. Soon after we left the huts they were detached to Delta Company at Grenay, until further reinforcements arrive to bring the battalion back up to full strength."

"Any idea how much farther we have to go from here to the houses we're meant to occupy?"

"We're nearly there—about half a mile according

to the sar'nt major. We're taking over the cellars below a row of ruined miners' cottages on the right-hand side of what used to be a street. He says that opposite there's a derelict church where it's believed the Germans are resident. Right, I'd better get back."

This was at least enough information to enable William to picture the conditions awaiting them. "Thanks for that. It helps us to be prepared. What are the arrangements for the handover then Andrew?"

"Most of the Princess Pats are already well on their way back to Bouvigny, and our paths probably crossed in the fog. I understand that they left a rear party of six to give cover, waiting for us to arrive. So we'd better get a move on, there's lots to be done before daybreak."

Andrew turned and then disappeared through the fog. The column started to move forward again, and William followed with 2 Section. They hadn't gone far before William almost bumped into Sar'nt Major MacKay.

"Follow the guide just to your right. I've already been to look at the cellars, and it's filthy, waterlogged, and mostly open to the elements. There are a good two or three inches of stagnant water on the floors, making it pretty tricky going underfoot. Be extra careful, as there's also some debris from the ceilings and adjoining walls. Apparently, Fritz has been shelling them almost nonstop during the past three weeks, and as a result they lost half of their original strength poor sods. With the heavy bombardment, as well as the heavy rain, I'd say they deserve a break back at the huts. Luckily for us, it's been pretty quiet here for the past three hours or so."

"It seems as though there's not much we can do until daylight then sir?"

"Not a great deal, no. But although it may be quiet at the moment, we still have to stay alert. The company commander has asked the Quartermaster to send up a supply of tarpaulin during the night so that we can at least get some overhead cover in case it rains again. If it does, at least the fog should clear, and then we can see what we're doing."

"We must be grateful for small mercies, I suppose sir."

"Best not to be too grateful Corporal. Anyway, company HQ, the medical orderly, and stretcher-bearers will go in first, followed by No. 1 section and then you next with number two. Any questions?"

Ten minutes later the column ahead moved again, so William followed on behind until they were stopped by a staff sar'nt from the Princess Pats who showed him down to the rear doorway of what little was left of the cellar in the first house.

William called back over his shoulder, "Careful as you go through the doorway."

Ahead of him William could hear a lot of cursing and sounds of splashing as the men in front struggled in the dark through the standing water, then someone at the far end lit a candle. Though it didn't help with the way forward, it did at least give them something to aim for. Then they lit a couple of oil lamps and everyone started work on banking the debris at the front wall; The lying rainwater was now slowly disappearing through drains that had been unblocked, and after an hour, the whole place was looking reasonably habitable.

CSM MacKay gave the place his blessing, sufficient to agree to release the Princess Pats people to set off for Bouvigny. Then 1 Section took over the watch duty at street level, while William's team continued the clearing up work.

Andrew came through from the third cellar. "William, come through here. I bet you've never seen anything like this before."

As they came face-to-face, Andrew's wide grin told William him he was about to see something that in the circumstances was about to make him laugh, "Oh yes, Andrew. What is it?"

"Come through here. The sar'nt major's in Cellar Four."

William followed him through to the third cellar and pulled him closer to the other side where there was an inner door frame, but nothing left of the supporting wall other than a few inches of skirting. The CSM could be seen studying a map at the table. William smiled at Andrew and then knocked on the door.

In reply, the sar'nt major poked his head through the non-existent wall, "Come in!" he smiled and raised his eyebrows.

Everyone in the cellars stopped work to see how William would react when he saw the door with no supporting walls; perhaps he would give them the reaction they were hoping for.

The sentries above, as well as any Germans nearby couldn't have been more surprised at the great howls of laughter that followed. This extraordinary breach of discipline was indeed a rare event, but on this occasion it provided a little light relief from the tension everyone was feeling.

By 0600 most had managed to make a reasonably dry spot to lie down and get some well-earned rest. But it wouldn't last long, as the bleary-eyed CSM was on the prowl. "Come on now. Look sharpish. Let's get the tarpaulin fixed above before our neighbours across the other side of no-man's land get organised. Then hopefully you can have as much sleep as you need in the remainder of today."

Each section had been given a sheet of the tarpaulin, which they started securing as a temporary "ceiling" above their respective cellars. Until this was completed late morning, they reverted to night-time sentry cover of one Lewis gunner and one from a rifle section.

Andrew came through from the third cellar just as William was arranging a sleeping bag and about to lie down on a pile of logs. "We're all finished for the time being, so I'm going to have a short break now William."

"I had the same idea. Remember that most of the platoon, including yourself, are at least twenty years younger than I am. I'm definitely feeling my age this morning."

As Andrew stepped back through to his section cellar, there was an explosion at street level, followed by two others in quick succession. Then Sid Walmsley opened up with the Lewis gun, although how effective it could be was questionable. All those who had tried to get some rest were now wide awake, on their feet, and rifles at the ready.

"Jimmy take Jack and Pat O'Connor and go up top to join the others. Don't forget your gas masks. The CSM warned me the Hun have started using new mustard gas shells. Pete, take Trenchard and set aside the ammo from the pile of boxes in the corner."

A short time later the CSM checked each cellar to see that everyone was okay. He sat next to William, "Damn. I got that one wrong, didn't I? Just when I was convinced the Germans were either absent or understrength. But maybe they've been reinforced overnight. Do you think?"

The exchange of artillery and small arms fire continued in bursts for the next three hours, the heaviest bombardment coming in their direction. The remains of what had been the gunners' and bombers' sections in the first cellar took a direct hit from a German trench mortar, killing all four members of the section.

Their time in the cellars at St-Édouard continued with daily exchanges of small arms fire and, on a couple of occasions, a heavy coal box shell. With though two days remaining before the next move, as if they were making a special farewell gesture, the Germans opened fire with more Yellow Cross gas shells just after 1700 hours.

Fortunately, the whole company had already been stood to and ordered to put their respirators on.

However, despite being prepared, by about 2200 hours William was feeling increasingly short of breath and couldn't seem to get rid of an irritating cough. As he was already aware, these conditions were often associated with gas poisoning, so Jimmy went through to the HQ cellar and returned with CSM MacKay and the medical orderly.

The medic took one look at William and concluded that it must be a case of gas poisoning, "Doesn't look too bad though. Nevertheless, we'd better have you seen at the RAS to be on the safe side. In any case, you won't be fit for anything for at least two days I'd say."

This last advice didn't register with William; he felt so unwell, so weak. Hopewell and Burns helped him through the back door of the cellar and followed the Orderly the short distance to the regimental aid station tent. The MO took one look at William and then nodded to the Orderly. "Another one to add to the list Corporal. That's nine walking wounded, eight gas cases, Andrews with the head wound, and the two critical chest injuries on stretchers. Let's get them back to the Crest Farm dressing station as soon as possible."

CHAPTER 16

Close Encounter with Fritz

AN HOUR LATER, two open-topped ambulance trucks arrived outside the RAS. The two stretcher cases were carefully loaded onto the open back and then William and three others were seated on the side benches either side of the stretchers. The others got on to the back of the second truck.

The journey to Crest Farm took nearly an hour and a half. The poor road surfaces, together with parts that were quite congested, made William half expect them to end up in a ditch on a number of occasions. The two guys on stretchers looked to be in a pretty bad way. And by the time they pulled up outside the ADS, they had stopped moving or making any sound; it didn't look good.

An orderly took one look and waved William and the other "walking wounded" down. A medical officer then appeared and checked out the two on the stretchers and then beckoned the orderly. "They've gone I'm afraid."

In reception, William was seen by a nursing sister, "'Corporal Gregory? 25th Battalion Cape Breton Highlanders?"

"Yes Sister," he replied. "I'm Sister MacIntosh. Bed rest for a few days. And with some fresh air, we'll soon have you back to your unit. As you've spent most of your life in the mines, it's not surprising you should have bronchial symptoms. Nurse Lei here will get you bedded down in the outside area with the other non-surgical cases."

"Thank you for your help Sister, and to you also Nurse" William replied.

Sister MacIntosh handed William's notes back to Nurse Lei and then moved on to other patients.

"Pleased to be looking after you Corporal Gregory. As Sister says my name is Lei Lin, and I've been nursing here for the past twelve months, there is one other Chinese nurse here at ADS."

William's shortness of breath and coughing continued through that first night, but thankfully, didn't get any worse. He did sleep quite well and woke only every couple of hours, and whenever he did wake and looked around Nurse Lei was always sitting facing the row of beds. *Perhaps she never sleeps?* he wondered.

After an application of ammonia and with the plentiful supply of food and hot drinks over the next three days, he began to feel much better. Late morning on the fourth day, a medical officer doing his rounds stopped and examined William. He then turned to Nurse Lei, "How's the breathing and the cough, Nurse?"

"Much improved sir. The fresh air and rest seemed to be the solution."

"I think the symptoms indicate something more general in nature, not necessarily all the result of gas, although I'm pretty sure it has had an affect. I've seen several patients in the hospital at Gouy who have been badly affected by gas, but in this case I'd say it's more likely to have been caused either by contaminated water, food, or the legacy of working in the mines all his life. I think he should be good to return to his unit tomorrow."

The following morning at ten o'clock, Nurse Lei and Sister came to see William. Nurse handed him a pile of freshly laundered uniform and his boots, "These are clean replacements for you to wear, and your personal things are in this small parcel."

"Many thanks Nurse. Thank you again, Sister."

Sister smiled and held out her hand, "Here you are, best not forget this, it was in your jacket pocket. No rifle, so you may need it." She gave him back the C96 Mauser pistol, complete with its holster. "Transport has been arranged for 1200 hours to take you to the Brigade MT Pound, and you will rejoin the battalion from there."

As promised, the vehicle arrived a little after noon, by which time William was dressed and ready for the road. He got up into the cab next to the driver, who wanted to talk, whereas William felt more like taking time out for a sleep. However, the driver continued to chat, "You probably don't know, but yesterday Bravo Company moved again—to St-Laurent much closer to Lens. I'm only taking you as far as the Brigade MT yard, and they will tell you where you go from there."

As they drew nearer to the Lens sector, the sound of a heavy artillery duel grew increasingly louder by the moment.

At the entrance to the MT Pound, the driver stopped and leaned out to speak to an MP and then turned back to William, "Okay. They know where the 25th Battalion is located. They will direct you from here. Good luck now."

William shook the driver's hand, "Well, thanks for the lift."

The driver waved as he drove back out through the gates.

William now looked around the yard, which showed little sign of life other than a tented workshop and three vehicles. The MP manning the gate put a hand on William's shoulder and pointed up the track leading south-east, "The 25th Battalion has just moved about one and a half miles up the track straight ahead, close to the church spire. Can you see it?"

"Yes, I can. What's there other than the church?" asked William.

"Well, I was up there yesterday, and there's a sandbagged sangar near to the battalion headquarters. The sentry will direct you where to go from there. It's half five now, so you'd better get a move on before dusk settles in. Be careful up there, the battalion and German lines are very close to each other, and there have been a number of clashes in the area in the past few hours."

William started out up the track, and after a few yards he turned and looked back toward the MT compound. The MP waved after him and called out, "Keep your head down now. And good luck."

"Nice that," William muttered under his breath. "Everyone wishes you good luck as if they know something I don't."

In his mind he mulled over the situation he now found himself in—how alone and vulnerable he was. "The only thing I have to protect myself is the Mauser, and I've no way of knowing whether it's still capable of firing."

What used to be a track was very rough underfoot, making it slow going up the hill. He stopped every couple of hundred yards or so to catch his breath and to check his bearing by the church spire.

Although the sound of shellfire was some way off, there was sporadic small arms and machine gun fire much nearer. For sure if a German patrol came across a lone Canadian, he wouldn't stand a chance.

With dusk fast approaching, when he last checked his watch only a few minutes ago, it was half past six. So he'd now been marching for nearly an hour, and the church spire was barely visible in the gloom. Soon it would be dark.

Suddenly, the relative quiet was interrupted by the sound of an approaching vehicle, although he couldn't be sure from which direction. As the sound of the engine grew nearer, he quickly looked around for somewhere to hide. Luckily, a couple of yards on his left there was a shell hole by the side of the track, so he slid into it and crouched as low as he could in the bottom.

The vehicle stopped what must have been only yards away, and the driver left the engine running. The cab door opened and then closed again. William held his breath, listening carefully.

Then, in deep guttural tones, clearly German, and only two or three yards away. He caught snatches of the conversation, which he understood to be something about Canadian patrols near St-Laurent. Then all went quiet once more.

William's heart was pounding. At any moment, they would find him for sure and the memory of Major MacLeod's warning in Witley came flooding back, "Never allow yourself to be taken prisoner by the Germans."

The sound of heavy boots came nearer and then stopped directly above his head. This was it then, the end. How on earth they didn't look down and see him William would forever count as one of life's mysteries.

There was a brief exchange now between two voices but this time not so clear. "Ja, Kapitan," was all William gathered when the second person obviously replied to his officer.

It sounded as though they had turned and started walking away from the edge of the shell hole. William could breathe once more.

He reached inside his jacket, slid the Mauser out of its holster, and took a quick look over the top. All he could see was the back of two Hun walking towards the vehicle and a third standing in the back of the open-topped armoured car.

Luckily, they were more or less grouped together in his line of sight so that he simply couldn't miss, provided of course that the pistol worked. There was only one way to find out, and William didn't hesitate. In a second, he was on his feet, firing until he had emptied the whole magazine, and all three Germans had fallen.

William was stunned at how quickly his first face-to-face contact with the enemy was over, and that the pistol had worked perfectly! He was rooted to the spot, hardly believing what he had just done.

After a good five minutes, he cautiously approached the vehicle. Here he was, stranded in an area known to be used by both sides, and with a German armoured car, and all three occupants now appearing to be dead.

William looked firstly at the Fritz lying face down a yard or so from the half-opened driver's door. The gold braid on his hat showed that he was an officer. He next leaned over the driver and turned the ignition key to off. Then finally, he went round the other side to his third victim, and was horrified to see the face of a young boy, probably not much older than his own son John who was now nearly twelve. "Damn them" he cried, "How can they send young children out to die like this?"

William sank to the ground, totally exhausted. He stretched his legs out and leant back against the wheel arch of the armoured car. He was overwhelmed by the desperate situation he found himself in— alone and in an area known to be frequently used by the enemy, and unsure of how near or far he was from the safety of the trenches occupied by the 25th Battalion.

With what little strength was left to William rapidly draining from every bone in his body, his eyelids grew heavy as he drifted into a deep sleep.

Searching for Gregory

Captain McInnis had just returned from a briefing by the commanding officer, and as he entered the dugout, a tired looking CSM MacKay looked anxiously for the latest news, "What's the latest then sir?"

"We're staying put for tonight at least Sar'nt Major. But there was some pretty disturbing news of Corporal Gregory."

"I was wondering what had happened to him."

"Apparently he was discharged from the ADS early this morning and virtually abandoned at Brigade MT. All we know from there is that he set off on foot in this direction, unarmed. That's the last anyone has heard of him."

The sar'nt major was on his feet and banged his fist on the table, "We can't just leave it at that sir. He could be anywhere between the MT yard and here, and without any means of defending himself if he comes across."

"Exactly what the CO said too. He's absolutely furious that one of our own should be treated so badly. He insisted that we do everything possible to find Corporal Gregory and bring him back. Apart from this shocking business, we can ill afford to lose such a highly respected NCO."

"I'm familiar with the track between the Brigade MT Pound and here sir. And provided he took his bearing on the church spire, it shouldn't be too difficult to find him—that is of course, unless he's been taken prisoner."

"That makes sense, Sar'nt Major. We must move quickly to find him and ensure his safe return. You should go with me together with Spellman and Makinson, they're such close friends. It's too dark now, so I suggest we leave at 0415 in time to catch first light."

The sky was overcast as dawn broke, but at least it was dry. The search party had been scouring the countryside for a little over half an hour when Captain McInnis pointed and called out, "Look, over there! Put your foot down driver."

Ten minutes later, the truck came to a halt alongside the German vehicle. William sat up and grinning from ear to ear with relief at seeing all his old friends once more—something he'd thought he would never see again.

He was still very weak from the efforts of the past twenty-four hours, but it didn't take much longer than half an hour before he was in the Cooper Trench dugout, and tucking into a mess tin of hot bully beef stew and tea.

Peter Spellman wasn't on watch for another hour, so he sat with William to make sure he was fed and then rested, "Thanks Pete. That's never tasted so good before. I'll be back to normal in a couple of hours."

"Well we'll see what the MO says before you start rushing things," Pete replied.

After an hour's sleep, William was really feeling much better, and was dressing when the CSM came in to check how he was doing. He also took the chance to bring William up to speed with what had been happening in his absence. "As you can see we're now in Cooper Trench, facing directly across to the Cité St-Laurent suburb. After they wheeled you off to the Crest Farm Dressing Station all hell broke loose. We were very badly beaten up by the German mortars, coal boxes, as well as gas. Mark you, our own artillery gave much the same in return.

"I suppose we must have been in the thick of the exchanges for something like five hours, and it wasn't until we were able to take stock of the casualties that I began to realise how badly we'd suffered. Mr Bell was wounded; seven from 3 and 4 Platoons died after a direct hit gas attack; Number 1 Section is down to two; and from yours only Makinson, Spellman and Trenchard are left. Of the original machine gunners and bombers, only Walmsley and Hughes are still with us, so the two Lewis guns have been withdrawn and replaced by the one Vickers. Finally, only yesterday, both Tucker and the medic from company headquarters were wounded by a sniper."

William was shocked by the news of these terrible losses. The company had indeed taken a severe beating while he was at Crest Farm. Of course, this meant that including himself, 2 Section was now only three strong out of the original nine. William was devastated to learn that so many he'd grown so close to had gone. But in another sense, he was relieved to see that Jimmy, Peter, and Trenchard had survived. "With Mr Bell out of action who's taken his place, sir?"

"Well, I'm temporarily running the show. The platoon commander was hit in the left leg—luckily not too badly—and he's now at Crest Farm, although we can't know for how long. Must've been there when you were?"

"I suppose he must have been, but there were so many."

"Anyway, it's good to have you back, but just be sensible and don't overdo it. I'm off now to a briefing by the CO. I'll be back I guess in a couple of hours. In the meantime, everyone knows what's expected of them. Cheerio, Corporal Gregory."

"Thanks sir, I'll be having a rest. And as always,

Makinson and Spellman will keep an eye on things here."

Having sorted his personal belongings, William got back into his sleeping bag and slept soundly for over two hours. Pete woke him with a fresh mug of tea.

"Thanks Peter, I'm much improved now. The sar'nt major told me about the tough time you've all been going through. It's a reminder to treasure every moment left to us."

"I do. I do, Willum," Peter replied.

"I know Jimmy thinks the same as me—in that, before this, these things always seemed to affect others. But this time it's a little too close for comfort. It feels very personal now."

It was more than an hour later that CSM MacKay returned from the briefing. As he entered the dugout, he beckoned William to follow him through to the map table, "You look a good deal better since I left Corporal Gregory. I've spoken separately with the CO and he agrees that we have no option but to field just one rifle section of six. So, with two manning the Vickers plus myself, the total strength of 6 Platoon is now nine, whereas at one time we were over thirty.

"We've learned a great deal since the Somme and more recently Vimy Ridge, and the situation here looking out towards the high ground we know as Hill 70 is quite different from past experience, with regard to the disposition of the German forward elements.

"With the work done here, the battalion now has at least a roughly straight-facing trench system. As you know, there's about a hundred yards of no man's land before we reached the first of what were once streets of miners' cottages. They're not facing us in a straight line, and their trenches and dugouts are to be found wherever there's some cover.

"So, at zero hour which is 0425 on the fifteenth, we'll go over the top; crawl forward I reckon about five or six yards; then wait until we are all assembled and ready to advance towards their barbed wire. We've then got one helluva dirty job on our hands to root them out wherever we can find them.

"Our mission is to take their forward positions by 0500 hours. Then we will lie low and prepare to defend against their counter-attacks. Is that clear enough, do you think?"

William nodded in agreement. "Thanks sir, that all makes sense, and it's good to be able to explain the plan to the others."

"Right then Corporal Gregory, off you go. Make sure everyone gets as much rest as is possible."

14 August 1917

The day was relatively quiet, and the main activity from the German positions came in the form of clusters of three-inch mortar rounds fired at random intervals every hour, luckily with little effect.

That night after dark, twice after dark that night, a voice called out in flawless English over a megaphone, "Tommy Wigan Pals. We're waiting for you."

William was standing on the top rung of a trench ladder looking out for signs of movement across the way. This made him smile as he'd heard of it from a couple of new guys who'd been at Vimy. Whilst there was no movement in front, his attention was suddenly drawn to someone standing behind him.

It was Jimmy, "Did you hear that again William? It's probably as well Fritz doesn't really know what bad shape we're in. The sar'nt major came into the dugout a minute ago, and he says it's certainly spooked a few of the younger ones in the company. You'd think we might do something similar to the Germans. But then what would be the point? They haven't got any feelings.

"I couldn't seem to settle William, although Pete

is fast on, and snoring like a pig. By the way, the sar'nt major said he wants to see you inside."

William stepped down the ladder and made for the dugout doorway. As he did, he smiled to himself at the sound of the loud snoring from inside. It reminded him of the many occasions in the past when Jimmy, Peter, Hodson, and Clarke used to snore in unison. Sad to think that the barbershop quartet had now been reduced to a duo. Inside, he popped his head into where the sar'nt major was sat at the map table.

"Come in and bring Makinson with you. Oh, and bring your tin mugs with you."

William beckoned Jimmy over, and they both joined CSM MacKay.

"Come. Come on in and sit yourselves down." He reached on the shelf behind and brought out Mr Bell's bottle of cognac, filled the three mugs and passed one each back to both William and Jimmy. "What's turned out to be bad luck for Lieutenant Bell has at the same time been our good fortune. The platoon commander's bottle of cognac has to be finished tonight. Here's to your good health. And good luck on our way to Hill 70 tomorrow. What's left of Number 6 Platoon will be looking to the three of us to lead the way into what will be a bloody and damn frightening experience for us all."

They raised their mugs in silence and then downed the warming liquor.

CHAPTER 17

Battle of Hill 70

TONIGHT, INSTEAD OF changing sentries every two hours, the company commander had ordered that shifts would change every four hours so that the men would be able to have longer periods of sleep before stand-to at zero hour. Five men were resting in the dugout, and other than snoring it was a picture of utter contentment if ever there was one— the sleeping men seemingly oblivious of the dangers facing them shortly in no man's land. However, it was more likely the result of sheer exhaustion rather than the lack of fear of the horrors awaiting them.

By the light of a single candle William was browsing the entries in his diary, which had been few and far between in recent weeks. He couldn't sleep and kept thinking about Elizabeth and the children back home in Argyll Street. They were never far from his mind. It was gone three by the time he nodded off, sitting upright with his back resting against the wall.

15 August 1917

No sooner had he drifted off than he was woken to see the faces of Peter and Jimmy staring at him, "It's 0400 William. Stand-to in ten minutes. We have to make ready in good time before zero."

By 0410 hours, everyone was dressed and nervously checking their weapons and equipment. This repeated checking that everything was in order was more to relieve the building tension than the chance that anything had been misplaced or lost.

The weather had been warm and dry for the past five days, but now, signalling the approach of zero hour, it began to rain—a light drizzle of the kind that quickly soaks through to the skin.

William went back into the dugout to recover his groundsheet and caught the attention of Jimmy to pass the word on for everyone to do the same. The whole platoon was now assembled either in the trench or the dugout, and they were left with their own quiet thoughts, no doubt of loved ones back home.

A strange, eerie silence had descended on the

whole area and even the rats had stopped their otherwise constant squeaking. William filled in the time by checking the section's webbing straps and then, with a pat on the shoulder, returning to his place at the foot of the ladder. Farther along the trench to his right, William could clearly hear someone sobbing and muttering under his breath; another was repeatedly coughing; behind Peter Spellman, he could see Trenchard blessing himself and muttering the Lord's Prayer—surprising, as he had always said he was agnostic; and someone else was being violently sick.

The sar'nt major came out of the dugout and ordered "Fix bayonets."

The rattle from shaking hands fixing bayonets broke the silence, helping to relieve the tension. They were ready to go. William looked at his watch, it read 0425 hours—zero hour. This was it. He climbed to the top of the ladder and followed the CSM over the top, crawled forward, and waited for the others.

They lay still for a few minutes until the rest of the men were out of the trench and ready to move forward. CSM MacKay then got to his feet, and crouching, waved them all on. Then as though synchronised, the heavy guns on both sides opened fire at the same moment. There was a blinding flash, and William was blown off his feet. Dazed and half-buried by falling debris, he lay for what must have been nearly five minutes before he gathered his senses and turned on to his side. His ears were ringing from the effect of the explosion, and he could hardly hear a thing. He looked around and realised that he was lying alongside a deep shell hole and that the sar'nt major must have taken a direct hit.

He could see Peter and Jimmy looking in his direction, so he waved them forward. It took them a few minutes before they reached him. Then they both bent closer so that they could hear. Peter leaned over, "Are you hurt Willum?

William smiled and touched both their arms. He cupped his hand to his mouth, "My hearing's coming back slowly. The sar'nt major's gone, so we're just about all that's left. Pete, will you go back and check the rest and then let me know. I only hope that Sid Walmsley is still okay with his Lewis gun, although how much ammunition he might have left is anyone's guess. I think we should stay here for the time being and be ready to defend against any counter-attacks, which I expect will come before too long. So we just have to hope that Jimmy and I will be able to hold them off until you get back. Thank God Fritz doesn't know what bad shape we're in. At least we haven't used our rifle ammo, and I've also got the Mauser pistol as backup."

Luckily, the expected counter-attack didn't materialise in the next half hour, and eventually Peter returned, together with Sid, complete with the Lewis gun. They were now four in total, and it was obvious to William that, until reinforcements from the 24ᵗʰ Battalion caught up with them, there was little they could do to make any further progress. In the end it wasn't the 24ᵗʰ, but company HQ and Support Platoon who arrived at 1000 hours.

"Corporal Gregory?" The familiar voice of the Company 2IC Captain Forsyth who was the first to arrive.

"Yes sir. It's good to see you. We're all that's left of 6 Platoon."

"I'm so sorry to hear that. The CSM served with my father, you know. Major Harrington is keen to move forward as soon as possible, so you will have to tag along with Sar'nt Crawford and Support."

"We're just so relieved to see you, sir. It was looking pretty hopeless."

"Good to have you on board Corporal. I think it's better if the four of you from 6 Platoon stick together for the time being. Right. Let's go!"

They all stood, bent double, and set off at a slow

pace, their progress only hampered by the constant explosions of German trench mortars and the constant clatter of machine gunfire. The ground ahead was obscured by thick clouds of smoke.

After only about ten yards, William tripped and fell to his knees as he stumbled over a prone body. "William. Come on," urged Jimmy.

"Oh no!" William cried, frozen to the spot at the sight of Peter Spellman lying on his back, his blood-soaked hands holding his gut. He was choking and spewing great fountains of blood. William leant and put an arm around Pete's shoulder, lifting his face nearer to his. "Bear with it Pete. You'll be okay. Stretcher-bearer! Medic!" he yelled, but to no effect.

Pete's pale face stared back at William, and he still managed a weak smile. "We did well, didn't we, Willum? Showed them what the fighting MacKen ..." Then suddenly his eyes were still.

William bowed his head, tears streaming down his face. He gently rested his dear friend back to the ground. They had been through so much together. The overwhelming sadness he felt, the absolute futility of the slaughter all around them, was replaced by the anger and determination to avenge the death of Peter and so many of his good friends.

Jimmy grabbed William by the arm, "I know. Poor Pete. But we have to go."

They followed on after the support boys and eventually found shelter in a trench come shell hole recently abandoned by Fritz.

Captain Forsyth gathered everyone together. "We'll rest up here a while waiting for news of further reinforcements. But we must stay alert at all times. The darkening sky was lit by the occasional flares, mortars and small arms fire that continued all night.

16 August 1917

With the first glimmer of daylight, they were ready to continue the advance. Sid Walmsley had been hit in the shoulder late yesterday and had been moved back to the RAS during the night. Now it was down to William and Jimmy.

At 0500 hours the usual routine was followed, led by Sar'nt Crawford, "Fix bayonets!"

William and Jimmy clambered out of the trench. Then Jimmy turned back to pick up his extra ammunition sack. William was by now a good ten yards in front.

The German heavy machine guns opened fire again.

TERMINOLOGY

Page 8.   **Tommycans** were used by miners to carry their food rations while working at the pit. The term "Tommy" was originally used by Wellington at the time of Waterloo to describe the British Soldier.

Page 20.   The term "**prayters**" was used in Lancashire for potatoes.

Page 22.   The **beak** is a term used to describe a magistrate.

Page 24.   Lancashire was the centre of the cotton textile industry, primarily due to the fact that there were large numbers of skilled workers. Plus, there was a tradition of spinning and weaving in the area. The finished cotton goods were also transported by rail to Liverpool for export. Whenever problems arose, the expression "**trouble at t' mill**" was often used.

Various   German troops were at times variously referred to as 'the enemy', 'Germans', 'The Hun', or 'Fritz'

AFTERMATH

IT WAS THE long-established practice for the commanding officer to write a personal letter of condolence to the next of kin within a week of any fatality. But in this case, the numbers lost at Hill 70 were such that he had delegated the task to company commanders for other ranks. Captain McInnis's table was piled high with ID discs, pay books, and journals. He was making careful notes before passing the record to the company commander.

"Corporal Gregory sir, 6 Platoon Section Commander. As you know, he was a nice man who was respected by all ranks. I was particularly struck by the photograph with his family and the engraving on the back of his pocket watch which I think must have originally belonged to his father. There's also a bundle of personal letters to be returned to his next of kin, together with his other personal belongings."

Major Harrington looked through the items that

had belonged to William. 'Thanks, Alex. Very sad. Good man."

"Private Makinson is the only one left out of the whole of 6 Platoon. He's now in the hospital at Gouy."

The company commander continued to look through the items in front of him. In the back pocket of the pay book was the photograph of the Gregory family posing proudly outside their home—William, his wife Elizabeth, and their four children. He sighed, shook his head, took some ink on his pen nib, then began:

Dear Mrs Gregory,

It is with great sadness that I write to inform you that on Thursday 16 August 1917, your husband, 877776 Lance Corporal William Gregory, died as a result of wounds sustained in action at the Battle for Hill 70 on the outskirts of Lens.

EPILOGUE

WILLIAM IS BURIED in Plot H16 at the Communal Cemetery, Aix Noulette, Pas-de-Calais, on the Bully-Grenay Road. The Battle of Hill 70 was launched on 15 August 1917 and ended on 25 August. The action lasted eleven days and involved four Allied divisions under the command of Canadian Lieutenant General Sir Arthur Currie. The recorded Canadian casualties totalled 9,198 killed, wounded, or taken prisoner. The opposing German Empire forces consisted of five divisions who would otherwise have been deployed to the Third Battle of Ypres (Passchendaele). The Germans were commanded by General Otto von Below, and their casualties numbered 25,000 killed, wounded, or taken prisoner. Hill 70 is often referred to as the Canadians' Forgotten Battle.

William's widow Elizabeth remained in Canada and later moved to Toronto. She eventually remarried John Lupton.

Jimmy Makinson recovered from his wounds and returned to Aspull in 1920.

ABOUT THE AUTHOR

JOHN SYKES WRITES as Jon Moorthorpe and has previously written *The Gregory Journal* (2014) and an anthology of short stories, *Migrating Geese* (2015).

He was born in the mining village of Moorthorpe in Yorkshire in the early part of the Second World War. At the age of fourteen, he started work as a cub reporter on the local newspaper. He worked for a time for the NCB, and at nineteen, he enlisted in the Regular Army and served for fifteen years in the Coldstream Guards. After leaving the army, he worked in the aerospace/defence industry for over thirty years when he travelled widely throughout Europe, North and South America. He was chairman of the UK Equality for Veterans Association from 2009 to 2013. Today he continues to be actively involved in several Armed Forces charitable organisations.

John has four children, eight grandchildren, and one great-grandchild. He lives with his partner Jean in East Sussex.